The Green Line is the place where Jew fought Arab to a standstill in Israel's War of Independence in 1949. There was never any peace made in the wake of that war so the Green Line remained etched in the soil until washed away by the victories of the 1967 Six Day War. But it still remained. It is used as a reference point in negotiations between Israelis and Palestinians. For me it was the invisible border between two different dimensions.

To go over the Green Line was to enter the wild, wild Middle East.

BEYOND THE GREEN LINE

BEYOND THE GREEN LINE

Marc Goldberg

Published by Marc Goldberg in 2017

ISBN: 978-1-9998455-0-6

Designed and typeset by Mousemat Design Limited
www.mousematdesign.com

Printed and bound in Great Britain by Createspace www.createspace.com

There are some people whose love and support ensured that I achieved my goal of writing this memoir. Most importantly my wife Gali as well as family and friends I wouldn't have been able to do it without you. You know who you are.

This book is dedicated to the bold, brave and beautiful guys of Orev Tzanhanim August 2002.

I have changed the names of all the people I served with. In many cases the people are composites of many of the guys I served with. To write about each of them individually would have lead to an unwieldy manuscript that didn't do justice to the events. Everything that I have written about happened. Events I have written about that occurred in the West Bank took place between August 2002 and August 2004. In places I have collapsed the events of several different operations into one operation for brevity and narrative purposes.

Contents

Prologue

JENIN, WEST BANK, ISRAELI OCCUPIED TERRITORY

We'd had a tough climb up the hill but it had been worth it to keep us hidden. At the top it was a different story. Anyone looking up from their window would see us on the crest silhouetted against the moonlit sky. I could hear other small teams working in Jenin that night; each engaged in their own private firefight. The snap, crackle and pop of their gunfire reverberated around the city. A minute after setting up we came under fire too.

It was the pinging on the rocks that gave the game away. I was surprised by how quickly the enemy fire erupted. It wasn't particularly heavy, a few guys with rifles, but they were quick on the trigger. I peered through my scope to locate the source of the firing only to see what looked like someone signalling in Morse code with a torch. While I was puzzling out why they were signalling I heard more pinging on the rocks around me. It wasn't Morse code – it was muzzle flashes. The people I was looking at weren't messaging me they were shooting at me.

The major asked our sniper if he had a fix on the location of the gunfire. He hadn't. He then turned to Uzi, the spotter. Uzi had a clearer view through his own equipment and he directed the sniper and the nine of us onto the targets. The range finder classed them as being 550m away, within effective range of the sniper's M24 rifle. It also put them outside the effective range of my own weapon. Whereas my scope amplified by only four times, the sniper's magnified by six. He still couldn't see anything, but I could. The terrorists were firing from the window of an apartment building. They looked like green ghosts as I spied on them through my scope. There was more than one but I couldn't quite make out how many. "Ehud, have you got them in your sights?" Uzi asked the sniper.

"No," came the reply.

Uzi then began another patient explanation via prominent landmarks to guide him towards his targets: "Do you see the tree at the foot of the hill?" he asked.

"Yes."

"Do you see the second lamp post on the main street running into the city?"

"Yes."

"Do you see the apartment building right next to it?"

"Uh-huh."

"Do you see the window on the fourth floor above the ground with the terrorists hanging out of it, shooting?"

"No."

What the fuck? I pulled my eye away from the viewfinder to stare at Ehud. Bullets were still ricocheting off the rocks. I tried to make myself part of the ground while maintaining my view of the enemy. I couldn't understand how they were able to range in on us at this distance. The pinging was close by. I wanted to shoot back. Instead I peered at my enemy as I waited for the order. Even if I did open fire they were too far away for me to hit them.

The major told Uzi to mark the target with an infrared laser. I saw the laser beamed onto the target through my own scope. The major turned to the sniper, addressing him by name. "Ehud, how does it look now?"

"I see the laser but not the target itself," came the reply. I was having kittens. I had wanted to go to sniper school more than anything but they hadn't sent me. The reason was obvious: unlike Ehud I had 20/20 vision.

Finally, the enemy was in the cross hairs and he was going

to get away because this idiot was blind as a bat. Ehud was the only sniper not on training at that particular time and he wore the strongest prescription lenses known to man. To make matters worse, he couldn't wear his glasses whilst peering into the viewfinder of the scope. "Just fire at the laser on my command!" The major said. I figured his ability to keep calm at moments like that was the reason for his rank. I'd never been angry with the Palestinians, though I was prepared to shoot at them, but I would have throttled Ehud at that moment. I couldn't understand why everyone else seemed to be so damn calm.

The major spoke: "Everyone fire together on my command." The target was 550m away from us; the maximum effective range I had fired at using my M4 rifle was 250m. But I wasn't prepared to turn down the opportunity to fire a shot in anger. The major gave the order and we opened up, each of us firing one shot. Through the eerie green on black of my night scope I saw the enemy duck and move away from the window. Probably shaken but still alive.

I was upset. Everything had been perfect. Maximum effective range for a sniper at night is 600m and yet Ehud had missed. The major turned to Uzi. "Well?"

"One puff of smoke on the wall about a half metre below the window," Uzi reported.

The major looked at me. "Marc, do you know the ballistics of your weapon at 550 metres?"

"Yeah," I replied defensively. Was he going to try to blame me for this debacle?

"So where do you aim?" he asked, a smile on his face.

"Above the target," I replied. "Way, way above the target," I muttered under my breath. I shot an evil glance at Ehud. How could he have missed?

A machine-gun opened up somewhere deeper inside Jenin. Perhaps another unit was having more luck than we were – or maybe less. The enemy had been right there in my cross hairs, in all of our cross hairs, and we had been impotent. He had survived. The major didn't seem to mind that the terrorists had managed to get away. He fairly cackled with glee. "Let them see how it feels to be shot at!" he remarked. I was silent. One shot each was all we fired that night. The bad guys had disappeared.

No one else shared my feelings. No one else cared. I wanted to go back and do it again, to actually kill some of them, and said as much to the major when we were back on the base. He told me we were done with Jenin and heading back to Nablus.

1

THE BEGINNING

My story doesn't really start in Jenin. It starts 23 years before. My name's Marc Goldberg. I'm a Jew born in the Jewish part of London to Jewish parents who gave me the most Jewish name it was possible to give a kid at the time. Marc. Growing up I knew so many other Jewish Marcs and Marks that everyone called me Goldberg; if they didn't, twenty kids would turn around whenever a teacher called my name.

At the age of 13 I had my bar Mitzvah. I became a man. A very small one, admittedly. I moved to a new school in the heart of London, the City of London School for Boys. A very expensive school, a very big school filled with other, bigger "men". I hated every moment of the three years I was there. My grades went from being As and Bs at my previous school to Ds and Es at this new one. I didn't make friends. I have one memory about my first year there. The other kids made a makeshift ring for themselves in the classroom and one by one each of them would go in and fight someone else of a similar size. I refused to go in the ring. I refused to stick up for myself throughout the time I was there. My self-esteem dropped away to nothing.

The school had two main staircases, both of which led to the fifth floor where all the science labs were. If you kept going up one of them you came to the caretaker's apartment; if you went up the other you came to a little annex where the staircase suddenly ended. This was my sanctuary in that school. There I sat most break times reading stories of soldiers and assassins and spies. I read about British Paratroopers in World War Two. I read about the SAS and other commandos. I read books during lessons too when I could get away with it. I did everything I could to escape the shirt and tie reality of this big school an hour's train ride away from my home. It wasn't school, it was prison, and I was stuck there until I was old enough for it to end.

My youth movement was a different story. There I learned about leadership, I learned about my people, about the Holocaust, about Israel and the rebirth of a nation. Whereas all the stories I learned in Hebrew school about the Jews had happened thousands of years ago the stories about Israel were happening right now. I found an outlet there, a place where I was more than just the little guy being pushed around. I rose through their hierarchy to a leadership position. I lived for that youth movement. It was the antithesis of school.

In the summer of my sixteenth year my youth movement took me away to Israel. It was my first time there since the age of five. Two things happened on that trip that made me think Israel had something going for it. The first was seeing a religious guy run across the street in Jerusalem to catch a bus. He wore a skullcap and the white tassels from his tsit tsit were swinging free and proud for all to see. My initial thought was that the guy was pretty brave to flaunt his Judaism in public followed by the realisation that everyone there was Jewish so it didn't matter. When you've spent your whole life being a part of the smallest, most minuscule minority, when the highest compliment a non-Jewish kid at school can give is "you don't look Jewish"; understanding that you're in a place where your minority status no longer exists was a shock to my worldview.

The second shock was seeing all the soldiers. They were all Jews. It was crazy. I was this little "man" who daydreamed all day of killing Nazis while experiencing a reality of being pushed around by people bigger than myself. Now I was in this land where Jews wore uniforms and carried guns. They wouldn't have taken shit from anyone. I wanted that power, that confidence. I wanted to be a Jewish hero like them. That was it.

At the age of 16, I decided to become a soldier in the IDF, the Israel Defense Forces. When I hit eighteen, I spent a year in Israel with my youth movement. I studied Jewish rebirth after World War Two. School was done. I had been waiting for the prison sentence to end for five years and I had made it. In that year I decided I was too immature to move to Israel quite yet. Instead I managed to get a place at Manchester Metropolitan University to study History. While there I realised I had a head for studying and excelled at learning for the first time. But I hated Britain. I was a Jew in the United Kingdom who felt like an outcast. I felt distinctly un-British, apart from the general populace, a member of a tiny minority that didn't fall into the British class system, that was distinctly not posh but not working class either.

I looked at Jewish politicians as sell-outs who had chosen a British identity over a Jewish one. It seemed impossible to me to be both. I felt like an outsider in the country where I was born and a total sense of belonging to a country I had barely even visited before the age of fifteen. My year in Israel was in 1997. I returned to a Labour-run government in Britain – the first of my lifetime. I didn't care. It mattered far more who the government of the state of Israel was. The leanings of the people in Westminster felt as relevant to me as the leanings of the people in power on Mars. I looked around me at the United Kingdom and saw a place where Jews were a hated minority without a voice. A place with a government that didn't care about me or my people. I was what they call an angry young man on a quest for an identity and I had glimpsed it in the Jewish state.

2

2001: MANCHESTER METROPOLITAN UNIVERSITY

Back in the 1990s the big buzzwords were 'management consultancy' and the big firms all had representatives visiting universities offering graduates loads of money to work for them. I watched a girl leave Manchester Metropolitan's Geoffrey Manton building; she had curly black hair and was wearing woollen gloves and a thick jacket to protect her from the Manchester weather. She was clutching a treasure trove of corporate bullshit under her arm while chatting to a friend on her mobile phone.

I slouched on the wall outside trying to urge myself to go into the recruitment fair. I imagined row upon row of banks, management consultancies and other corporate entities selling their wares to the graduates of the mediocre Manchester Metropolitan University. As I saw it, their graduate schemes offered a life of middle-class anonymity. All of them standing there with their best smiles on handing out prospectuses to students thinking only about how much money they were going to make. There had to be more to life. And there was: just a plane ride away Israel was waiting for me. Still, a part of me doubted. Could I really do this? Could I really go to Israel and join the army? Was it even possible?

The time had come to make it happen or let the dreams die the death of so many adolescent dreams. l knew going to Israel wasn't a logical choice but it was the only thing I wanted to do. Where the thought of working in a corporate empire filled me with dread, the thought of achieving my ambition of becoming a Paratrooper in the IDF filled me with joy. Therefore there was no real choice. If I didn't go to Israel I would have spent the rest of my life wondering what might have been.

For three years I had felt guilty knowing that an Israeli my age was serving his country in uniform, that he was sitting somewhere in Lebanon killing and being killed for his people while I was getting alternatively drunk then stoned and occasionally turning up to lectures. The time had come for me to play my part. My plan was simple. I'd begin my military career in a unit called Sayeret Tzanhanim and end up as Chief of Staff of the IDF. Broken down into little steps it seemed possible. Step number 1 was to get myself out to Israel and become a citizen; step 2 to get into the army; and every step after that could take care of itself. Or so I told myself.

3

TELLING THE PARENTS

"Hi Mum and Dad, as soon as I graduate I am going to live in Israel and join the Israeli army … I'm going to become a general." My parents were sitting at the breakfast table in their dressing gowns. My dad had just put his usual bite-size piece of Cheddar on his toast and my mother had taken a carefully crafted segment of grapefruit onto her spoon. Mum looked at me with a faint smile before looking at Dad. He just stared at me, toast halfway to his mouth.

"Where has this come from all of a sudden?" he stuttered, my mum put her hand on his forearm.

"I've been talking about it for at least three years now, Dad!" I was instantly impatient with him. Hadn't I prepared him well enough for this? I had been talking about it for a long time. He may not have believed me – I may not have believed it – but I had definitely told anyone who would listen that I was going.

Mum was calmer; she had a smile on her face and didn't say a word against it. "He has mentioned it a few times, darling." I was surprised. Mum was an unlikely ally. We looked alike and had the same fiery temperament; any arguments in the house had usually been between us. She had spent a couple of months living in Israel before I was born; the only reason she hadn't stayed was because she met my dad while back in London on holiday. With her in my corner I knew that Dad would come around to the idea.

Once my mind was made I just wanted to get out. The process was pretty simple. I needed a stamp in my British passport that said I was leaving and to fill out some papers with the Jewish Agency in London. Once that was completed I was good to go. While searching online about making Aliyah I stumbled across a language school that offered rooms for its students. The course was five months long and promised to offer a soft landing to new immigrants (they helped new people open a bank account and deal with government bureaucracy). When I saw that the course started in mid-July, just after my graduation, I felt providence was lending me a hand. I booked myself on the course and prepared to turn my back on what felt like a pre-planned middle-class life in the UK to open a chapter that would set me on my path to becoming a Jewish hero. I was going to become another Moshe Dayan or Ariel Sharon, only better.

*   *   *

It was July 2001. The Second Intifada had been building up for almost a year. The month I arrived there were two suicide bombings but the Intifada was nowhere near its crescendo. In February of that year Ariel Sharon, hero of Israel, replaced Ehud Barak, another hero of Israel, as Prime Minister. The peace agreements that would come to be collectively known as the Oslo Accords had finally run out of steam. The failure of the head of the Palestinian Authority Yasser Arafat to conclude a deal with Ehud Barak signalled the end of Barak's career. It also marked the end of left-wing ascendancy in Israeli politics. The dream of Israelis and Palestinians living together in peace became a nightmare of death in the streets.

The moment the plane landed in Israel a bomb exploded in my chest. It was around six in the morning. I had refused to look behind me when walking through passport control; I hadn't wanted to see my parent's faces as I left them. The flight has disappeared from memory, entirely dwarfed by the enormity of emotion that fell on me when the wheels hit the tarmac at Ben Gurion International Airport. That was when the world collapsed on top of me.

I was in Israel, I was far away from friends, family and home, so why? Dreams of joining the Paratroopers? Of becoming a general in the army? The absurdity of these hopes hit me full force while the aircraft taxied along the runway. Now it felt too late; I was stranded in this strange place with nothing more than childish notions of becoming a warrior. I had cheated myself, I had made a huge and terrible mistake, committing to something I didn't understand for reasons I couldn't fathom.

The rest of the day was tough. Instead of the joy of moving to Israel that I had expected to feel I was just freaking out about what was happening. The Jewish Agency had arranged for someone to meet me at the airport and fill out all the necessary paperwork. I signed what I was handed to sign as if on autopilot. The body ignored the screaming voice in my head that was saying, no, wait, it's all been a mistake – I need to go home now!

I went through the motions. The rep from the Jewish Agency put me in a cab to Jerusalem and the language school that was to be my home for my first five months in the Holy Land as an Israeli. All the while, the same question reverberated around my head:

What have I done?

What have I done?

I had the whole day to think about the series of decisions that had led me to the Ulpan Etzion language school in the Baka neighbourhood of Jerusalem. I walked in to the registration room where a whole bunch of other new immigrants were waiting their turn to register with the school. I remember entering the room and feeling like all heads turned to look at me at the same time. I stood in the doorway and firmly placed a fixed smile across my face, but that was the only move I could get myself to make. Crossing the threshold and taking a seat like all the others seemed to be too great an act of will. I was standing there smiling at this room full of strangers unable to say anything and with legs that didn't seem to want to move. So I moved my hand and waved at them instead. I stood in the door smiling and waving at them. This lasted until an administrator spoke to me asking me to come in and forcing me from my numbness.

As I approached her I said, in a voice hoarse with the sound of instant failure, "I think I've made a mistake. I want to go home."

She looked at me and said, "You don't have to stay. You can do anything you want." A small part of the weight that had dropped on my brain lifted.

That night I made the call home, I spoke to my parents letting them know I had made a mistake and would be returning to their loving embrace. My mother calmed me down, "The course lasts five months, why don't you give it a chance? You can come back whenever you like." I remained unconvinced; we continued talking until we had decided that I might be able to stand it for a week. A week was long enough to take it for a month and a month long enough to start thinking that just maybe becoming an IDF Paratrooper wasn't such a crazy idea.

4

THE END OF ONE LIFE, THE BEGINNING
OF A NEW ONE

I arrived in Israel to be a part of the smallest class that the Ulpan Etzion language school had ever had. The school was older than the state of Israel. To be a part of the smallest class they had ever had was a sobering indication of the state of the country I had just moved to.

Less than a month after my arrival, a bomb went off in a pizza parlour in central Jerusalem. I felt removed from it, as though it was happening in a different country. Some of the other guys living in Ulpan Etzion took it really hard, though, especially the Americans. A pregnant American woman had been killed in the blast and some of them had known her. In total 15 people were killed and another 130 were wounded in that bombing.

My parents assured me that so long as I called them after an attack to let them know I was okay they wouldn't worry about me. With this in mind I went to one of the two payphones in the building to call home. The phone rang and a world away my mum answered. "Hi, Mum," I tried to keep my voice upbeat.

"Hi, darling how are you? How are you feeling about everything?"

"Yeah I'm okay, listen, relax, don't freak out or anything … a bomb has gone off, but I'm fine."

There was a pause on the other end, "Marc?" she inquired.

"Yes, Mum?"

"I want you to get on a plane right now and come home,

enough of this, it's too dangerous!"

"But Mum, what about all that stuff you said about me just calling you and letting you know I was fine? Here I am calling and I'm fine!"

"That wasn't the same! Don't you understand? It's dangerous!"

It was the last time I told her about a bomb going off. From that moment on if she didn't call I figured she just didn't know that anything had happened. Soon there would be too many bombs to keep track of anyway.

5

ENLISTMENT

There were two other guys on my language course looking to sign up to the army. Dave was from Canada and Sean from Miami. Sean and I were roommates. He was an amateur body builder with a law degree and just as motivated to go into the army as I was. Much as I tried to convince him of the greatness of the Paratroopers he had his heart set on tanks. Dave was a skinny guy who kept his head buried in a book. When he did peep out of it it was usually to utter something about how Israel was besieged on all sides by enemies and it was the duty of Jews everywhere to protect her. He was all fire and brimstone and didn't much care where he served just so long as it was in a combat unit.

After figuring out where the recruitment office was the three of us trotted down. In Jerusalem the central army office was in a crowded part of the city; it was dilapidated and guarded by a very bored pair of 19-year-old girls wearing battle dress and carrying M16s. They glanced at our ID cards and waved us in.

Inside I found a bustle of young soldier girls wandering around carrying papers, overcrowded desks with documents falling off the edges and all kinds of people in civilian clothes there for reasons none of them looked happy about. We were shunted onto some metal chairs and given various forms to fill out. The three of us sat in a row opposite an anaemic looking Hassidic kid. There was nothing to him but pasty white skin and bones. He clutched a book that he swayed into and out of while learning. Occasionally he would survey the room furtively, eyes peering out through his glasses. I guessed he was there to get out of his army service. After a couple of minutes one of the many doors opened and an older Hassid walked out, smiling, with an NCO. The beaming Hassid shook the soldier's hand, moved over to the anaemic kid, patted him on the shoulder and they both left.

The NCO then beckoned to the three of us to follow him into a small office. His English was awful and our Hebrew no better. He took the forms we had filled out and looked over them while we remained silent. He was a bald man with dark skin – I took him for a Moroccan – he was wearing glasses and had a big paunch. He peered at me through his thick lenses. It appeared to be my form he held in his hands. "You want sree munts?" he growled at me.

"Err, no I want to serve properly," I squeaked.

"What you want dis for? Take six munts!"

"No, I want to serve!" I looked upon it as a test. It had to be – there was no way that this guy was really trying to talk me out of joining the army …

"Okay, okay, two years." He typed something into his computer and a moment later a young girl walked in with a form. He put it in front of me and I signed before my nerves or my senses could interfere.

He took the form and slid it into a manila folder that disappeared into a stack of other files like it on his desk. I had become just another anonymous folder among thousands of others. The sergeant squinted through his thick glasses into the computer screen, clicked his mouse and a moment later the same girl came back into his office with another sheet of paper. The sergeant slid the paper over to Sean. Sean looked at the paper, picked up the pen and signed.

The sergeant reached for the paper, at which point Sean pulled it closer to his eyes for another look. "So, uh, how long am I serving for?" he quizzed.

"Two years, you serve two," came the reply.

"And erm …" he shifted uncomfortably in his seat. I looked at him with a sinking feeling in my stomach. He had turned pale. "What if I want to do one year?"

The sergeant looked up, confused, "So, you can do one year," he says.

"Hmm yeah, I think one year sounds much better … in fact, I'll just take the form home and think about it."

Next up was Dave, the holy warrior, convinced that as in blood and fire did Israel fall, so in blood and fire will Israel rise. I looked at him; he was younger than me, meaning that he had to serve three years whether he wanted to or not. For the third time the soldier girl walked in with the form. For the third time the sergeant handed it over. For the third time someone who could barely speak Hebrew turned green as he held it in his hands. He looked at the sergeant who was waiting with all the anticipation of a man who had no idea that his job was to get people into the army rather than keep them out.

David signed the form and I sighed a sweet sigh of relief. David's confidential file was open and the form had almost reached its final resting place with all the others when, in perfect Hebrew, he blurted out a string of words I didn't understand. The sergeant said, "Ok," picked up the form and ripped it up in front of us.

I was on my own, two years of my life signed away in the blink of an eye. I looked at the other two but said nothing.

Cheers, guys.

A month later I was awoken in the afternoon by my mobile phone ringing. (Though I continued living at the Ulpan I'd abandoned the daily Hebrew lessons in favour of the nightlife Jerusalem had to offer. It wasn't unusual for me to sleep at just about any hour of the day.) It was my grandfather. He was telling me a plane had crashed into one of the Twin Towers in New York. I had never been to New York and didn't really understand what he meant. I tried to shrug him off so I could go back to sleep but he was insistent something was happening, so I went into the TV room downstairs to see if there was anything on the news.

People were there crying as I sat down and watched the images of smoke billowing out of what had been one of the icons of the New York skyline. Then I watched another plane fly into the second tower and I was no longer in Israel. I wasn't even in the 21st century. I was in Sarajevo, it was 1914 and I was watching Archduke Franz Ferdinand being assassinated. The world was changing before my eyes. The stable world I had grown up in crumbled along with those towers and I watched it happen live on CNN.

I sat in that chair watching the news with my mouth open along with millions of other people all over the world. I stayed there until the evening and then went for a run. I tried to work out what had happened. The feeling of witnessing the end of the world I had known and the beginning of a new one never left me. I was on my way into the Israeli army with the object of becoming a Paratrooper. If I succeeded I would fight those who hated me because of my existence. There was no room in this world for Jews, they said. Those who attacked America agreed with them. I felt like I was in the right place at the right time doing the right thing.

*　　*　　*

When the language course finished I moved from Jerusalem to Tel Aviv and spent most of my time bumming around, waiting for my call up to the army. My family came out to the port city of Eilat, in Israel's south, for Passover and I took the bus down to join them. While sitting in a luxury resort I watched the aftermath of a hotel bombing on the news and was aware that the Intifada had moved up a notch. As my family and I had been celebrating Jewish freedom from slavery in Eilat a suicide bomber walked into the festive meal that was taking place at a hotel in the coastal town of Netanya. There he detonated his suitcase bomb killing 30 people and wounding another 140. The press called it the Park Hotel massacre.

Two days later the Israel Defense Forces moved into the West Bank in full force to attack terror organisations at source. Operation Defensive Shield, as it was known, marked the end of any cooperation between Israelis and Palestinians. It also marked the moment the IDF started to use everything in its arsenal to attack Palestinian terror. The Palestinian leader Yasser Arafat was left besieged in his Ramallah compound, the Muqata. This siege would be lifted and then resumed several times during my service, ultimately ending when Arafat went to Paris to die in 2004. As someone wanting to be an elite soldier the only thing that scared me was that all the fighting would finish without me getting a chance to play my part in it. I needn't have worried; my request to attend the gibush (selection) for the Paratroopers had been approved.

Gibush: Paratroopers Selection

It was my first exposure to the smell of canvas that was to dominate my army service; the first time I wore the green fatigues of a soldier; the first time I tasted army food. The night before selection, I lay on an army cot in an open tent thinking about how alone I was. Listening to the other recruits talking to each other made me wish I had bothered to attend more Hebrew lessons at Ulpan Etzion. I realised my fellow candidates knew just what was waiting for us. Their friends, brothers, fathers and all manner of other family members and acquaintances had schooled them in what to do and how to behave. I had only myself, and the willpower that had got me this far.

I was woken up at around four in the morning and put into a group with 20 others. We spent several hours running around doing all kinds of physical activities. I loved it. Months of exercise had all been for this, fuelled by the same dreams that had put me on a plane to Israel and had kept me going through school. I'd worked out hard and was ready to give it everything I had.

The gibush itself was easy, embarrassingly so. There had been plenty of running around, sometimes with a pack on my back and a stretcher run to finish it all off. Maybe one or two people quit my group but that was it. I surprised myself by feeling glad to see them go; it gave me more confidence to carry on. After a few hours of physical testing it was all over and I was on my way home, high as a kite having conquered the dreaded paratroopers test in style.

A few weeks later I received a letter from the army telling me

I'd passed and could expect to be conscripted straight into the Paratroopers. I was stunned. My plan was working. My thoughts turned beyond training to officer school and the long career that awaited me in the IDF. I knew there was one more challenge before I could say I was really on my path to success: the next gibush, the selection to the famed reconnaissance commandos of the IDF – Sayeret Tzanhanim. This was the real test. Another letter arrived in the post not long after: my official draft into the army. My date was set for late August 2002.

I was finally going in!

7

August 2002 "Bakum": IDF Central Administrative Base

~

The officer chewed a pencil as he leaned back in his chair, eyes transfixed by the contents of the file he held in his hands. Inside the file was all the data the army held on me. It consisted of a single page and was the results from an IQ test I had done that day in the recruitment centre in Jerusalem, as well as my results from Paratrooper selection. He looked from the file to me and, still leaning back in his chair, dropped a bombshell. "You passed the gibush to the paratroopers but you're not going. There's no more room."

I sat there, mouth open, palms dripping with sweat. "But … but … but … I came from London to be in the Tzanhanim," I croaked. My tongue seemed to stick in my mouth.

"Yeah, well there is no room so I am going to give you a bunch of other options."

"No! I don't want to hear any other options! I'm not interested in any other options!" The words fell out of my mouth in perfect Hebrew before I could even engage my brain. My throat constricted, eyes hurting with tears being held back. His eyes narrowed. I tried another tack. "Please … if there's no room I need your help, we have to figure out a way to make sure that there is room. Can't they just throw another bunk in a room somewhere? You see I don't just want to be in Tzanhanim, I want to be in Sayeret Tzanhanim!" If I had thought that my revelation would make a difference to this man, I was mistaken. He clearly hadn't understood that the future Chief of Staff was sitting before him. I had been firm and I had begged; surely one of those must have helped.

I remembered a talk we had been given about the army while I was on ulpan. A skinny American with a scraggly beard had spoken to us about the intricacies of army bureaucracy. He told us about his nephew who had been desperate to get into the Golani reconnaissance unit but had been denied and thrown to the Nahal brigade instead. His nephew refused to consider any of the other options and insisted on going to Golani. In Israel insisting on getting your own way often works. I remembered a conversation with a kid on my gibush who told me that the army is just a slave market that slings people to the left or to the right without rhyme or reason and that you have to fight to get what you want. So I decided to fight the army to get what I wanted. I looked at it as a second, unofficial gibush. But instead of shouting and screaming in the Israeli way I decided to be very British and polite about it.

The officer sent me outside and told me I would be called back at the appropriate time. He might have sent me away but I never left his side. When he left his office, I was waiting there to remind him that I was the English guy he was helping into the Tzanhanim. When he went to eat, I was there sitting opposite him reminding him that I was the English guy who passed the gibush and could he please help me into the Tzanhanim? I waited outside his office until the shadows became so long they merged with one another, darkness fell and the lights around the base came on. I was in limbo.

I watched as other new soldiers went into his office and came out, each time wondering if I would be called in next to be told that I was going to be a paratrooper after all. I was scared that the two years I had given up for the army were going to be a complete waste of time. I waited and waited but still I hadn't got the call. Then the officer stepped out of his office and saw me sitting there in the same chair I had been allocated hours before.

"Oh, you still here?" I looked at him, utterly dejected. He turned to his assistant. "Send him to Camp C," he told his clerk.

Camp C? Camp C didn't sound anything like Tzanhanim to me. It wasn't. Camp C was where all the soldiers the army hadn't been able to place were sent. I was stuck with the various odds and sods who hadn't been assigned. I could hear music and see lights coming from the other side of the base; someone said it was a show being put on for the new recruits to the Paratroopers. With that comforting knowledge I crawled into a sleeping bag, surrounded by people I didn't know, and fell asleep.

The next day I was summoned before the same officer. When I sat down he had a smug look on his face and was biting the end of a brand new pencil. Sitting next to him was an officer with three bars on his shoulder denoting the rank of captain. More importantly, he had the red beret of the paratroopers tucked into the left epaulet of his olive coloured shirt. The officer said to me, "Tell him what you told me yesterday," and so I began my pleas to fulfil my journey towards the vaunted paratroopers of my dreams.

When it was over, the two men opposite me looked at one another and then asked me to leave. I was none the wiser as to how well my pleas carried with the two men. I was put in a line with some of the guys who had been in Camp C. At the end of the line people were assigned to their various units. As I waited I heard someone say, "I hope they send me to a unit where I can go home every weekend." The voice was high-pitched, nasal and right behind me.

I reached the end of the line to find a soldier sitting at a table. Without looking up at me he simply asked for my army number. I gave it to him.

"Goldberg?" he asked.

"Yes," I said, my voice already shaking with emotion, fatigue and stress. Was the plan already shattered into pieces?

"Tzanhanim," he said and pointed to a group of soldiers

standing next to an old bus. Anyone watching would have seen me walk towards that bus just like anyone else. But inside my head was a different story entirely. I was walking towards the achievement of my only ambition. I was going to be a Paratrooper. I was going to join the ranks of the men who had jumped into the Mitla Pass in 1956, of the men who liberated the Old City of Jerusalem in 1967 and the veterans of countless other battles. I was going to become the man I had dreamed of becoming all those years ago in the little annex at the top of the school steps. The child was no more. A paratrooper was replacing him.

I had done it!

8

TROM TYRANUT

I knew nothing about what awaited me. I imagined it would resemble the war films I had seen and expected to find a drill sergeant who would spend the next several months shouting at me like in the film Full Metal Jacket. When the bus taking me from the Bakum arrived at the training base the Paratrooper on the bus got up and said in a tired voice, "Ok, we're here. Grab your stuff and wait in the camp."

And that was it; for hours, nothing happened. No shouting, no bullying, no nothing. The Israelis didn't go in for any of that stuff. Unknown to me boot camp hadn't even started yet. I was in pre-boot camp; a soft landing to give new recruits the chance to get used to wearing a uniform, and to be assigned to their specific units. Despite my fears of the unknown and the pounding in my chest, I still wanted to get to the Special Forces.

Those of us who had requested the gibush for special units were taken away to the edge of the base. We had each brought with us a bag with a shovel, a one-man tent and two water canteens. There were a couple of hundred of us and we were split into groups of about 15 to 20 people. We all stood there as our names were read out and one by one we were given a group number and sent in the direction of the soldiers who would be directing our selection. I moved silently over to the knot of fighters who were standing next to a number 19 that had been written on a piece of cardboard and attached to the chain link fence on the edge of the base. I stood there waiting as, one by one, the other wannabe Special Forces fighters arrived at my group.

I wondered if the instructors would beat me, or starve me and I was certain they wouldn't let me sleep for the three days of testing. I stood waiting in the darkness of the pre-dawn desert at the edge of the camp next to a chain link fence, aware that my fate was in my own hands. There would be no excuses if I didn't make it to the Sayeret because the only person who cared whether I made it to the unit was me.

The first thing that happened was that our watches were taken from us. With that small action completed we marched out of the base and into the Judean Desert. It was August and even the nights were hot. Once we were away from the base the gibush began. Looking left and right, all I saw was competition for the limited number of places available for my dream unit.

I was trying to get used to the fact that no one was shouting at us or imposing themselves or the tasks on us. The guy running the gibush simply told us what to do and offered us the opportunity not to do it. For one task he told us all to run to a rock and back in 30 seconds. He counted down and when I heard him reach "one!" I was off like lightning, made it to the rock and was one of the first back. I took care to make sure that the same people were standing to my left and right. It took more than 40 seconds before everyone was back in position. I know because the instructor showed us his stopwatch. "Not very good … again!" And we were off once more to the rock. I reached it and ran back again and again and again. I inhaled desert dust kicked into the air by the others and my throat was soon dry as we continued on and on in the same way, never quite hitting 30 seconds.

I don't know how many times we ran before he stopped us, "What's the problem?" he asked, "Is it too hard? Why can't you do it?" A couple of excuses came from the assembled wannabes. I didn't dare speak; afraid my poor knowledge of Hebrew would adversely influence my chances of getting through. I'll never know how long we spent running to the same rock. At some point the instructors started talking. "Who wants to sit this one out?" a big man said while eating a chocolate brownie. "It won't mean anything bad," he added.

There were no takers and off we all went once again. Soon the offers were more subtle: "Who wants to do push-ups by the side as the others run to the rock and back?" Off we went, though this time two of our group were doing push-ups while waiting for us to return. I knew they were finished. They hadn't been thrown out of the gibush, but these guys were already taking the easy option and the instructors were watching.

"Fill up your water bottles and drink!" barked the little man. "This time you are going to make it in 30 seconds, believe me," he said as we consumed the lukewarm water in our bottles. It was as much a relief for the break as it was to get rid of the dust that had turned the inside of my mouth into a desert.

He positioned us back into the original three lines and allowed the two fighters to sit by the side and continue their push-ups. He ordered us out again and as one we ran, hit the rock and came back in our original positions. He clicked down on the stopwatch and showed to all of us in turn as we stood there. "See, you can do it!" he said. The timer said 29.87 seconds. It was counter-intuitive; we were more tired than before but we had become more organised. We had, silently, almost subconsciously marked out a specific route to take and a way to get back into formation without bumping into each other.

The two doing push-ups never re-joined our group and sat at the side as we stood in our three lines. The big man took out a plastic bag and handed out numbered tags. Seeing them made my heart sink; my efforts to impress these older warriors had been pointless. They hadn't even been writing down scores for any of us. The tag was placed on my shoulder. It was number 12 and that was my name for the rest of the gibush. That was when the instructors pulled out their notebooks and started paying attention to who we were and how we behaved.

I wasn't touched, no one ever shouted at me, it was simply a case of do as you're told or sit out. I didn't just want to finish I wanted to excel. It was the first time I ever remember being determined to do well at something. All my life I had felt like an underachiever. I had suffered the humiliation of staring at an exam paper without knowing the answers to the questions too many times, but here, in the gibush, I had the answers. All I had to do was keep pushing through, be the first, be the most motivated. Everyone who quit was making it more of a certainty that I would be accepted.

My attitude towards the gibush changed after a conversation with one of the guys in my group on the first night during sleep time. This in itself was a surprise. I had prepared myself to be awake the whole time but they strictly gave us six hours of sleep per night. I shared a two-man tent with number 8. We spoke in whispers and he told me all about the mindset of the gibush. The instructors weren't looking for the fittest people, he said, but for those who helped out the most. The instructors were standing over us while we ate to see who made food for others and who just made it for themselves. He told me they knew we would all become fit through the training that awaited us. They were looking for who could still think even when they were exhausted.

I could now see the point of the running challenge: the fact that I had made it back in time had not been relevant; the fact that I hadn't helped the slower guys was. I changed my strategy. Now I was the helper guy. I wasn't running in front of the pack, I was helping someone slower than me. I encouraged the others on and did all I could to propel them forward. By doing so I was helping to get myself into the Sayeret. This was a theme for the army; helping others helps you, go alone and you're finished.

Each night, I slept in a tent with number 8 who schooled me a little bit more before we both passed out. There were no bestial soldiers and there were no beatings during the three-day gibush. I slept and I ate. This had been the big exam and I hadn't let up, not once. The whole way through I had been thinking of the Sayeret, imagining how awful failure would have felt, remembering the recruitment fair in the Geoffrey Manton building back in Manchester, remembering how far I'd already come.

After an easy gibush I proceeded to fuck up the interview completely.

9

THE INTERVIEW

That I was having an interview at all came as a surprise. As far as I was aware the gibush was my interview. Once it was all over, the men who had been instructing us and making notes on us shared a little about themselves and dropped the barriers that had existed between us over the past three days. Most importantly for me, they told us what units they had been in and when they had served. I knew that they were impressed with me. My lack of Hebrew hadn't harmed my chances – if anything, it had increased them, as the instructors knew my gibush had been harder than everyone else's as a result.

When my turn came to be interviewed I was led away from the guys I had been with for the past three days and told to sit on a bench in front of a green tent. There was a dark-skinned kid with bushy eyebrows already there waiting. There was just enough time for him to tell me his name was Avi before he was called into the tent and I was left on my own.

The only other interview I could remember passing was for a job with Sony selling TVs one summer. I doubted the experience would be of much use here. "You're almost there Marc," I told myself while I sat on that bench. Then the gesticulations of a reservist shook me from my reverie.

It was my turn.

Waiting for me inside were five reservists, a representative of each of the units looking at the new recruits. One of them had been running my team on the gibush. He was a very big, very bald man who now, for some reason, was wearing a cowboy hat.

The others all looked a lot younger. Some of them wore T-shirts with their unit insignia on them, though I didn't recognise which units they were. The interview began when the cowboy leaned forward and said, "Marc, what can we do with you? You don't even speak Hebrew?"

"Ah crap", I thought.

I have to admit that a part of me expected them to bow down in admiration at the fact that I'd come all the way from London to put my life on the line for their country. I simply blurted out, "Within a couple of months of army service I'll be fluent."

Someone else leaned in: "But why are you here?"

I answered that it had been my dream to serve in Sayeret Tzanhanim. He dismissed this with a flick of his rather large wrist, "Why is that your dream, Marc?" he asked quietly. They were all looking at me. I didn't know what to say. I was back on the top floor in City of London School for Boys. Alone and unsure of myself.

How could I tell these guys that I had come to Israel with visions of glory and to become the ultimate Jewish warrior? I had to say something that made sense to them. With suicide bombers blowing themselves up in Israel's heartland I hadn't expected anyone to ask what I was doing there, certainly not anyone in the army.

"This is the best army in the world. The only one that is willing to look after Jews," was the line I came up with. I looked at their faces and I could see that they were unimpressed. I fidgeted in my seat.

"So do you just want to kill an Arab or something?" asked someone else. He was wearing a cap with one of the unfamiliar unit insignia on it.

"No," I blurted out, painfully aware that the people I wanted to impress more than anything were wondering if I was a psycho. "If I'm going to spend two years in the army I just want to make sure I serve in the best unit I can," I said with as much confidence as I could muster. But what I really wanted to say was that Israel was every bit as much my home as it was theirs and I wanted to protect it. But I felt too embarrassed to say so. Those words felt naïve. So I said what I thought they wanted to hear. The mood relaxed somewhat and the big guy gave a small grin and looked at the soldier to his left. Perhaps they felt awkward too; perhaps they just thought that a young man who had no idea what he was getting into had walked into their tent.

Then they started with questions about my choice of unit. "Why Sayeret Tzanhanim, Marc? You know there are other units too? Would you consider going to a unit other than the Sayeret?" I told them this was the unit I wanted, the best unit in the army, and the reason I had come to Israel. But inside I wasn't so sure any more. If I gave the wrong answer they might not send me to any of the units,

"Sayeret Tzanhanim is of course my first choice but you guys are the ones who know most about the army and I will go where I am sent," I said. Heads nodded and I felt pleased that I had said something that provoked a relatively positive response.

After a couple more questions they released me. Their questions had caught me off guard, especially the one about just wanting to kill an Arab. I knew killing was inevitable for a soldier but my motivation was to be the best, to be special. Killing someone hadn't featured in my mind as a reason for joining the army. The interview marked the end of the gibush; the adrenaline in my system was gone and my eyes attempted to close themselves despite my brain telling them to remain open. I was in the hands of the army now and the army would decide my fate.

Once the interviews were over we were led back to our camp, which was really just a collection of canvas tents. Someone let out a loud whistle, someone else let out a cheer and then the whole camp was applauding those of us who walked back in.

They cheered us all. This was the mindset of the Israelis, always encouraging each other, always lending a hand. I looked around at the guys who hadn't done the gibush, none of whom I knew, and felt the sense of belonging that had so eluded me in England. I found my bunk and dumped my gear on it, then stumbled my way to the shower before crawling into a sleeping bag and passing out.

At 6 a.m. the next day I stood in a line with all the other guys who had successfully completed the gibush and watched an officer read out names and units from his list. My fists were clenched and I repeated over and over in my head "Sayeret, Sayeret". Perhaps thinking if I whispered the word to myself enough they would let me in. "Please God and the spirits up high, please just send me to the place I have to be," was my prayer.

The officer looked up as he took a breath. He went back to his list and read off some more names, before, finally I heard "Goldberg". "Here," I said, still silently praying, fists clenched, eyes closed, voice in my head whispering Sayeret, Sayeret, and then I heard it … "Orev."

What the FUCK was he talking about?!

It couldn't be! I felt the tears forming. Orev? No, no, he had said the wrong unit. He had got it all mixed up! He must have. This was the only challenge in my life that I had truly worked for, truly aspired to, worked my arse off for and wanted more than I had ever wanted anything. I would have paid any price, done anything they had asked of me. I had spent day after day wanting, envisaging, dreaming and thinking about the fucking Sayeret and doing all in my power to get into that mystical unit. And I had still failed!

The idea of being a member of the famed Sayeret had so utterly consumed me that I had never considered what to do if I didn't make it. I relived the gibush in my head, asking myself a million questions. What I had done wrong? What could I have done differently? What had they wanted to hear in the interview? There must have been something. But it didn't matter. The Orev was where the army had sent me and it was to the Orev that I would go.

10

Boot Camp Begins

I had rolled the dice and I had lost. The Sayeret had been denied to me and this other unit, this … Orev was to be my home. The army owned me and I was going to have to figure out how to live with the consequences of the decision they had made. Myself and the 19 other guys I had been thrown together with were directed to two large, ten-man tents with ten metal cots apiece and a small locker next to each. There were six tents in total to house all of the new soldiers being trained up and facing those tents were three more for the training staff. In between their tents and ours was a rectangular parade ground measuring about 20 by 40 meters and at the end of that stood a big tent that served as a dining room. Next to the dining tent stood a portable showering unit with the three showers and two toilets that over a hundred of us would be sharing. This area was known in Hebrew as the "plugah" which also means a company of soldiers.

There were a few people sitting on their cots chatting to one another at the far end of my tent but I had no interest in being friendly. I walked out of the tent fingering the mobile phone in my pocket, considering calling home and figuring out a way out of the army. Instead, I just sat down in an obscure part of the plugah feeling sorry for myself. I wasn't left to my own devices for very long. Above the cacophony of foreign voices I heard the familiar sound of my name. I looked around for the source and saw a swarthy, dark-skinned soldier wearing a red beret calling me.

I slowly got to my feet and went to find out whether there

had been a mistake and I was supposed to be in the Sayeret after all. "Marc Goldberg?" was all he said as I approached him. I nodded and he motioned for me to follow him. He moved around the back of the staff tents to where several tables and chairs were waiting. He introduced himself as my squad leader. His English was non-existent and my Hebrew was awful but we managed to struggle through a few of the basics.

He wanted to know if I was happy that I had been placed into the Orev and I nodded in the affirmative. What the hell else was I supposed to do? Tell him that my dreams had been crushed and that I considered myself a failure for being sent to his unit? In any case, I worried that if I said no they would simply throw me out of the Paratroopers. He explained that he was one of four staff members who would be training my team during boot camp. He was responsible for half the soldiers in the team and another squad leader bore responsibility for the other ten. Above him was my sergeant and above him my officer. Beyond the officer I didn't need to worry. The interview was mercifully brief. At the end he patted me on the shoulder and told me not to worry so much – that it would be ok. I wondered how he had been able to read my mind. It hadn't dawned on me that a mere year and a half before he had been sitting in my seat and remembered exactly how it felt to be in a new place and not know anyone.

My officer also interviewed me that day. He was a hulk of a man at over 6' tall, clearly not a person to be taken lightly. He motioned for me to sit down and introduced himself as my officer without giving me his name. "You're not to talk English anymore," he said and then he went on to tell me to work hard and that he was happy to have me in his team. Then he stopped talking. The short interview was over. Unlike my squad leader he never smiled, in fact he didn't betray a single iota of emotion at all. After an awkward silence I walked away from my interview only for him to call me back and tell me to salute him. After saluting … my officer I made my way back to the hustle and bustle of my new plugah. So far boot camp wasn't anything like I thought it would be – the drill sergeant of my nightmares and Hollywood never showed up. Instead all I had were my squad leader's smiles and my officer's distance. Meeting my officer actually made me feel a bit better. He looked like such a tough bastard that it made me think if he was in the Orev maybe it wasn't the second-class unit I thought it was.

The following days were more like a summer camp than the army. Sleeping in tents and running from lecture to lecture, none of which I understood. I didn't talk to anyone at first, it was difficult because of the language barrier but it wasn't just that. Every day I watched the new recruits to my beloved Sayeret strut around the plugah with their heads held high and every day I remembered my failure to join their ranks. They would say things to me like "Don't worry, the Orev is good too," and I would despise them for it.

There was a lot to do in those first days. We didn't have rifles yet and we were only slowly receiving the tools that we would need in order to fight. Our rifle magazines and equipment were signed for and we spent hours being instructed how to work on them to bring them up to standard. We would have to tape them up and put pieces of parachute cord on them to make it easier to pull them out of the equipment pouches on our battle dress. This was when I began to meet the guys I had been put with – as I met them I slowly forgot my need to belong to the Sayeret and began to believe in the Orev.

Training in boot camp was mostly divided into a series of one- and two-minute missions. We would all sit in a tent with the squad leader holding a stopwatch. He'd give an order saying, "Within one minute, you each must have taped up one magazine … Go!" There would be a rush around the tent as we all lunged for the tape to get the mission accomplished in the time available. There wasn't any time for shyness in this situation and I became adept at sign language in order to get what I wanted. At the end of each minute we would be sitting precisely where we had been at the start. If the mission wasn't complete we could request more time but we all had to be back where we started and sitting in silence at the end of the prescribed time. If not a punishment would follow. At first the punishments were nothing, we'd simply be told how important it was to be ready. Later, once the sergeant got involved, the punishments would really begin in earnest.

11

Sergeant Golan

The sergeant scared me. He wandered around the camp with an expression that said he was looking for a fight and a swagger that told you he could win it. He knew the effect he had and relished it. Once he saw me sitting on the side of the parade ground; the moment we made eye contact he skulked up to me, sticking his face directly in front of mine. "Marc!" he barked, "What the hell are you doing?!" I looked at him and feebly said, "Just sitting here." He looked me up and down before breaking out in a grin. "Great, have fun with that," he said before skulking off, leaving a bewildered British recruit still sitting down unsure as to whether or not he was in trouble.

Our officer had given the team one order so far and that had been that no one was permitted to talk to me in English, which meant no one spoke to me at all. I didn't want to get to know anyone anyway. They hardly looked like the superheroes I had expected of the legendary Israeli paratroopers. Instead of seeing tough soldiers, I only saw children, regular 18-year-olds who did not conform to my vision of the Paratroopers. I wanted to leave. I wanted to be in the Sayeret. I wanted to be left alone.

A small corner of the camp had been set aside for the smokers. It was in the smoking corner that I met people; it was the only place we could go and not be on the clock for the little missions we were always being given. The only times we were allowed to go there were meal times and in the free hour before we all had to be asleep. It was there that guys from all the different units gathered to share their stories of torment at the hands of the army. I didn't understand much of what they were saying but people there laughed so hard when I tried to speak Hebrew that they quickly accepted me. It wasn't great fun sitting there, watching people laughing at me, but they didn't seem to mean anything by it. In truth I was the one who had to adjust. When you're the odd one out you can accept it and go with it or rebel against it and go on your own. I chose to stop trying to do everything alone, to stop sulking about the fact that I wasn't in the Sayeret and most importantly to let go of all of the preconceptions I had fostered with regards to life in the IDF. I was rewarded by having a place to go to and people to talk to.

12

LIRAN & UZI

So Liran just came up to me one day and said, "Hey Brity, you're a funny guy … now we're friends and you're coming to my house for Rosh Hashanah, right?" It was the classic Israeli invitation. A statement rather than a question. I nodded my acceptance, kind of in shock. I knew Liran already, which is to say I knew who he was. He also spent his time in the smoking corner, he seemed to know everyone already and he was in the same squad as me but we had never exchanged any words. When I got to know him better I understood that Liran could have gone to any unit he wanted to. He chose to be in the Orev. I hadn't known that people chose Orev as their first choice and assumed everyone was a reject from the Sayeret or one of the other units. Knowing he was there out of choice was another reason for me to think that perhaps the Orev was a place worth being in.

Liran did a gibush that was the gateway for all the special forces units and intelligence units that don't have names and which no one is supposed to know about. After acing the physical tests he found himself in an interview being asked what he wanted to do during his military service. He just looked at them blankly and said, "I don't know." They sent him to the Paratroopers. That was typical of Liran; he just breezed through everything like it was no big deal. His dad was a retired officer; like a lot of the high-ranking officers he told his son not to go for a combat unit. He told him he had done enough fighting for the both of them. Liran signed up anyway and eventually he chose Orev because … well, why not?

Uzi was a baby-faced soldier who grew up in the same area as Liran and who was desperate to prove that despite his baby face he could make it through the training. Later on he would be nicknamed "Baby". He had a natural talent for finding out information, both during boot camp and throughout our army service. If I wanted to know what was going to happen in the next week I asked Uzi; if I wanted to know how to get hold of something I asked Uzi. When I became friends with Liran I became friends with Uzi at the same time, that's just the way it was. We'd eat together, we were in the same tent together and we were in the same squad too. So now I had gone from being alone to being one of three and the Orev was looking better all the time.

One day, around the time I started hanging out with Uzi and Liran, we were treated to a lecture from our officer, the big bastard who spoke softly and rarely. I wasn't yet allowed to know his name. I had to address him as "platoon commander". He had an unnerving way of looking at us – as if he wanted to hit us.

He spoke about the meaning of the word tzevet, or team. This word "tzevet" was holy in the IDF. The 20 of us who comprised the August 2002 intake to the Orev were now part of a tzevet and, as such, we were expected to help one another at every possible moment. We would be spending the rest of our army service together. We would endure all that the training staff would throw at us and then we would endure everything that the enemy would throw at us – and we would do it together. Unlike elsewhere in the IDF the members of August 2002 Orev Tzanhanim would remain as one organic team throughout their service.

That day, I signed off on a distinctly battered M16 assault rifle. Before being taken down to the rifle range we had to pass a qualification test. It was all in Hebrew, of course. I didn't have a chance at passing it, I could neither read nor understand anything. I looked down at the page. There were diagrams of the rifle with multiple-choice questions around them, all in Hebrew and therefore virtually illegible. I felt the tension rise within me. If I couldn't pass this then I couldn't go to the range with the others.

I barely heard the creak of the seat next to me as Golan occupied it. "How's it going?" he whispered in my ear. I tensed up, not knowing how to answer. I didn't have to. He put his finger next to one of the answers to the first question. I turned to him and he simply nodded his head back to the page. I circled the answer and his finger moved to another. My sergeant, who an hour before had made us all run around the base, stand to attention, then run around the base again because we hadn't swept the sand out of our tents (who ever succeeded in sweeping sand out of a tent in the desert?), was sitting next to me giving me the answers to the test.

When I had circled all the answers he rose and walked out; to my left the rest of my tzevet were staring at me. Later, once the tests had been marked, the sergeant read out the results. I had scored 100%. He insisted on playing out the charade to the end and started clapping. He glared at the others and they started clapping too. I was petrified everyone was now going to hate me; instead they were all patting my back as we left the room. We all knew what had happened but no one cared. This was my unofficial welcome to team August 2002 Orev Paratroopers.

The more boot camp progressed the less I cared about not being in the Sayeret. Golan worked us hard, far harder than the genial sergeant in charge of the Sayeret. And Golan's genius was that he always made sure the recruits to the Sayeret could see us being worked hard. Everyone knew he was tough, everyone knew we were working harder than anyone else. Which meant that we held our heads up higher than anyone else.

The tougher the training, the more it dawned on me I had made it into the kind of unit I had been trying to get into all along. I found pride in being with these guys and understood the gibush was just the first test and that completing training was by no means assured. A month into boot camp we'd already lost two of our number. I knew that with my lack of Hebrew I was going to be a burden unless I made an extra effort to help out. One thing I figured I could do was carry as much on my back as I could.

My opportunity to do so came during a forced march. There was one of these each week starting at just a few kilometres in length and culminating in the 90km march for our red berets after six months. These marches didn't scare me. I had run 10km a day while training for the gibush, so the 5km distance of our first march was laughable. The marches took place through the night. The first one saw us loaded down with our weapons, water and ammunition as well as one big radio, one stretcher and a jerrycan filled with 10 litres of water. Later, more pieces of equipment would be added but for the first march it was just these three. In keeping with my newfound ideology I opted to take the jerrycan.

The pace was a half-run half-walk, which stopped me from falling into a rhythm. My lower back was hurting after a few minutes. I couldn't help but breath in the dust kicked up by the boots of those in front of me. My mouth dried out and stayed that way. I was constantly looking at my watch to draw strength from each second that passed and yet I looked at it so often time seemed to stand still. The straps from the jerrycan bit into my flesh and the weight on my back pulled me down into the soft desert sand underfoot. Soon my face was wet not just with sweat but with tears. I didn't even possess the vocabulary to ask someone to take the load from me.

I wasn't the only one suffering. I could hear young soldiers crying out to stop for water or to be able to remove their load … just for a moment. I could hear them but they were in another dimension. I was locked inside my own world of pain and discomfort as I placed one foot after the other, praying the end would come soon. The struggle became one of internal desperation, constantly fighting with my body while failing to shut out the screams coming from within. The realisation that if I didn't get rid of the jerrycan I wasn't going to make it came all too quickly.

Before I knew it, I was shamelessly begging the new soldiers around me to take the weight from my back. I pounced on them one after the other begging them, using the few words of Hebrew that I knew jumbled up with my English. One after the other they waved me away, too encumbered with their own personal pain to help me with mine; "Pleeeeease," I begged, all restraints imposed by self-respect and dignity long since forgotten. The pain in my body completely dominated me. Eventually, I fell to my knees, only to hear someone behind me say, "Okay Brity, I'll take it." The joy that coursed through me on hearing these few words was one of the most wonderful feelings I had ever experienced. I shrugged the jerrycan off my back and allowed it to fall to the ground with a thud.

A smiling soldier picked it up. He gave me a playful punch in the arm, took the weight onto his back and moved off. I didn't yet know his name but he had shown me something I never could have understood if hadn't joined the army. It was my first experience of receiving a helping hand when I was in pain and it came from someone I didn't even know. The army would teach me what it was to be hungry, to be tired, to be in indescribable pain. The army would teach me how to balance those needs, to control my mind, even in the midst of suffering and how to be mindful of those around me whose need was greater than mine. They did it by making me feel the extremes of horror and the relief of help from a friend.

The sun rose over the dunes; our first march ended at the top of a steep hill. We walked up while the Sayeret walked down, having already completed their march. I bumped into one of the guys who had been in my group during the gibush. He nodded to me on his way down. "Don't worry, Brity, you've made it to the end!" I grunted back at him.

I turned to the soldier who was still carrying my jerrycan on his back. He wore a triumphant smile on his face. He nodded to me and I nodded back. A soldier fell to his knees and threw up. Golan walked up to him and patted him on the back as if throwing up was the best thing he'd ever done. The Israelis didn't mind if someone threw up or passed out on a march; for them it meant you had someone who was willing to push their bodies past what they were capable of.

This time it was Zacky who was throwing up. He had a 1st degree black belt in Tae Kwon-Do and slept in the cot next to mine. Every night when we were supposed to be asleep he whispered to me in broken English what we had covered in the lessons that day. While Zacky was being sick Golan took me aside, "Jerrycan?" he asked. I nodded towards the other soldier. He looked at me: "You finish with the pack you start with Marc, always!" It was somehow worse for the fact that he was saying it with a soft voice. He seemed so disappointed in me when he said it. There was nothing for me to say back. I just nodded and resolved to take a pack again and never give it up, no matter how much it hurt.

13

ELAD

We were hiding in a bush – Elad and I. We hadn't spoken before. We were supposed to have camouflaged ourselves by thickening out the bush with extra bits of shrubbery but we didn't bother. It was our first week in the field and we were only two days into it, yet the difficulty of the exercises, the lack of sleep and the language barrier had brought me to my end. I looked at Elad, attempting to keep the tears that were stinging my eyes from dripping down my face. Months of training remained and it was only going to get harder with each day. I told him everything, I poured my heart out to Elad there in that bush. The difficulty of being away from my family, my surprise at just about everything, from the lack of discipline to the lack of sleep and how tough the marches had been. Then I told him I couldn't hack it any more, that it had all been a mistake.

He played with the earth while I talked. He seemed to take it all in before looking at me with blank, uncomprehending eyes. He hadn't understood a single word I'd said. For a moment I just sat there staring at him before bursting into a fit of laughter; he joined me in suppressed hysterics as the two of us sat there in our bush.

That night I dreamed my tzevet were leaving without me. I could see the squad leader count them all and move everyone along. I tried to call out to them but the words wouldn't come so I jumped up from my bush to tell them to wait, waking up in the process. It was still dark and there was no movement, I was confused and afraid – almost too afraid – to go back to sleep in case the dream became a reality. I lowered myself back down into my temporary home and closed my eyes to dream of abandonment until it was time to wake up for real.

At the end of that first field week we were lined up facing the symbol of the Orev, a sword with wings on each side and cross hairs instead of a hilt. Golan set it all on fire. Once the ceremony was complete we followed our sergeant towards the cement fortifications of a nearby base. I took in the checkpoint in front of it, the raised pillboxes bearing down on the road and the barbed wire fence running along the side. There was a sense of foreboding about this base; here the soldiers needed these strong fortifications for their own safety. They lived knowing the enemy was nearby. This was the Paratroopers' advanced training base. Soon to be my home.

14

HELL – ADVANCED INFANTRY TRAINING

There was barely enough room for the 17 metal cots stuffed into a tent designed to house 10, but we managed. The tent was our home for three months of advanced infantry training. Our first night was spent on the base. The next night we had equipment on our backs and a stretcher loaded with boxes of bullets. We were on our way into the same dried up riverbeds and rocky hills that had made that first field week such a memorable experience. Three of the original number hadn't even made it through boot camp.

I remembered reading Menachem Begin's book *The Revolt* while I was enduring that place. At the time I didn't understand what he meant when he wrote:

> Whenever the foul reality of my surroundings forced itself on me I dreamt –not of the free world, not of a decent house, or a warm bath, or a walk in the woods, or of any of the boons given by freedom to a civilized human being. No! I dreamt of the cell in the prison, the barred cell, where there was company and my meagre mattress on the stone floor.

We spent most of our time in the dry riverbeds and hills surrounding the training base. The only place I dreamed about during those tough times was the tent and that miserable, forbidding base.

We spent our days and nights executing assaults on hills and then carrying the stretcher with a "wounded" member of the team around. The second week finished with a squad test. It consisted of moving across open ground, attacking an objective and moving while providing mutual cover. On the way, instructors threw riot gas grenades at us. The gas was green and thick. It didn't just make you shed tears but irritated the skin and caused pain in the lungs. It also stuck to anything nearby including cans of food and water bottles – just inviting some unsuspecting soldier to get the irritant on his skin.

By the time we reached 2 a.m. my squad was cruising; we had done all that was asked of us and had finished the final test.

"Fall wounded."

The command was directed at Oran, the biggest man in the tzevet. No one moved. We didn't understand; the test was over so why did Oran have to fall down wounded? "Have him on the stretcher in 10 seconds or I'll tell another person to go down and you'll carry him too," was the response to our silence. We scrambled to put him on the stretcher and lift it in the air. We moved over the dusty ground after our squad leader who was walking purposefully towards what appeared to be a large hill.

The hill was a mountain, twisted and jagged like the rocks it was composed of. The squad leader stopped at the foot of it and we stopped behind him. As one we stared up at this terror, instinctively knowing the task before us. The squad leader took a drink of water and looked at us blankly. We looked back pleadingly. He gave me a look of cold, calculated disgust. We were a mere irritation, a nothing. That simple look hammered it home. Being a paratrooper wasn't going to be easy.

The squad leader started up the thin trail towards the summit and we followed him. The path was narrow and in places blocked by large boulders. The stretcher had to be pushed, pulled, raised and lowered to make it onwards and upwards. There were times when we dropped the stretcher, complete with Oran attached, onto the rocks. The higher we climbed the tighter the path became until in some places it disappeared altogether.

I suffered all the way through. I suffered agony in my limbs as I pulled and pushed. I suffered the agony in my mind from the shock of thinking the night was over, only to be confronted by the evil of the stretcher and the darkness of the mountain. I remember being at the front of our little group screaming at the others to push as I pulled. A mixture of English and Hebrew and even Arabic curses escaped my lips. I remember hearing Elad chuckle behind me as he pushed at the other end. I silently marvelled at how he could laugh through all this. What mental toughness did the others have that allowed them to keep their composure. I shouted at Elad even more loudly and everyone started giggling as we lurched on with that damn stretcher ever higher.

Then other questions occurred to me on that rock: what kind of man was I that I could come all this way to carry a stretcher up a mountain in search of a red beret and silver parachute wings? What kind of man was I that I could urge these other men on even when I was at the point of exhaustion? And then it dawned on me that I might not be as weak as I'd thought.

We finished after the sun came up; the other half of the tzevet arrived just after us having come up via a different route. On reaching the summit we were told that a helicopter was on its way to pick up our "casualties" and that we had to find cover while we waited for it. I crouched down behind a rock and covered the way we had come. My sweat-soaked body shivered in the dawn as I fought to stay awake. Someone shouted "gas attack!" In the confusion of looking for our gas masks we forgot about the casualties still attached to their stretchers. It was only their familiar cry of pain as the gas grenades hissed that alerted us to their suffering. Of course the helicopters never came. Mercifully we were allowed to release our "wounded" comrades from their stretchers.

We were ordered to keep our gas masks on for the march

back to base. We moved down a very gentle slope on the other side of the mountain. That base was my saviour now; it marked the final resting point and the end of all that had gone before. But where was it? With each movement my Kevlar helmet pushed the clips of the mask deeper into my skull but I would never loosen the clips without being told. I plodded on with my skull aching. My breathing echoed inside the mask. My visibility was down to what I could see through two Perspex-covered holes.

The more we walked the greater the strain. The thought that the exercise was over kept going through my mind. It was unfair: we were done and yet they were forcing us to do more. Why? Tears rolled down my cheeks. I screamed and shouted and raged within the confines of that Perspex and rubber prison. The pain in my skull grew in intensity along with my frustration. It just never ended. Now, with the sun high in the sky and a night of endurance behind me, the army was demanding still more from me. It wasn't fair! How could I be expected to just keep on like this?

I continued to put one foot in front of the other. The pain continued, as did I until the base loomed large before me. We came to a halt. Standing there in a group I wondered what would happen if someone covered the air inlet to my gas mask. As I contemplated this, a hand came from beyond my vision and did precisely that. Starved of oxygen for only a second I wheeled around on the attacker. This was the last straw and it broke the camel's back. I launched my strike on the offender with a kick, followed up by punches. I didn't get very far as, once again, the sound of laughter, precisely when I didn't expect it, permeated through my mask. I had attacked the wrong person.

It had been Elad who had covered the mask, but with my vision obscured, I had missed him and dived on Sahar. The look of confusion on Sahar's face made me aware of my mistake while the laughter coming from Elad left me in no doubt as to who the real culprit had been. Hurt and confused, I removed my own mask and stepped quietly back into the fold, allowing the squad leader to be the centre of attention. He looked at me then shook his head suddenly as if to shrug off my little "incident" and said something like, "Nicely done, it was a tough night and you came through it well, now we are going to finish the way paratroopers always finish, with the stretchers out and on the run!"

I was going to kill him! We had just spent the whole night dragging the bloody thing up a mountain and now we had to open it again just to "finish the way paratroopers always finish". He looked back at me and said, "Marc, get on the stretcher." I practically collapsed onto that blessed/cursed thing and felt the thrill of a paratrooper stretcher run from the VIP position.

15

THE ONLY GOOD ARAB IS A DEAD ARAB

For the other guys "home" was everything that the word suggested. For me, however, it was an empty apartment. The others were always going on about Mama's cooking and catching up with friends; when I went back to my flat I usually fell asleep straight away and then took myself off to a bar called Mike's Place, where, too shy to actually talk to anyone, I got drunk and passed out on the beach. I'd wake up the next day wondering why I had bothered while patting down my pockets to make sure my valuables hadn't been stolen as I'd been lying there.

This weekend Liran had told me that there was already a plan and that I was coming. To that end I found myself standing outside my apartment on Ben Yehuda Street right near Tel Aviv beach waiting for him to pick me up. The thing is, I was the outsider on the team and I needed their friendship a lot more than they needed mine. Someone had told me early on that your tzevet was everything and you had to give them everything. For me that meant when out of the army too. So even though I was tired and aching I went out anyway.

Liran pulled up in his dad's car and we headed off to Friday night dinner at his aunt and uncle's house. Liran's parents were sitting inside talking to their family and two other middle-aged couples. They all seemed to jump up when we walked in, everyone was smiling and warm hugs by way of introduction were plentiful. The table was already filled with hummus, tachina and other Middle Eastern delicacies. Liran's aunt ushered me to my seat at the table and his uncle read out the blessings over the wine and the bread before we sat and began to eat.

Talk turned to a recent terrorist attack. A mother and her two sons – one 5 years old and the other only 4 – were murdered in their kibbutz along with another Kibbutznik. The woman sitting across from me looked straight into my eyes and said: "I'm utterly right wing. As far as I'm concerned the only good Arab is a dead Arab." I flinched. You're not supposed to say things like that; you're not even supposed to think them. But I knew that she had children in the army. I knew that her family was in Israel because when they were kids her parents had put her and her brother onto a boat from Morocco to Israel to escape rampaging hordes. Their parents followed several years later. She had reason to hate. I didn't.

16

INTO THE SLIPSTREAM

In pre-dawn darkness we scurried around getting our gear with the knowledge that our first jump into the abyss was upon us. Once dressed, we assembled at the hangar where the parachutes packed by pretty girls were distributed to us. We murmured to one another while we waited, shuffling along as, one by one, each of us took possession of a parachute rig. Buses were waiting to take us to the air force base next door. We drove around the base for about 20 minutes before stopping next to the Hercules aircraft that were to drop us over the sand dunes.

We were safely deposited by the side of a runway next to a small corrugated iron shelter; then we put on our rigs and stood there waiting. Dawn had broken and the guys were chatting excitedly. For some it was to be their first time on a plane. After a while a van pulled up and a couple of air force guys pulled out a trestle table and loaded it with bread, cheeses, yoghurt, vegetables and a huge flask of hot, sweet tea.

The others tucked in but somehow the thought of being dropped out of a big aeroplane from 300m up put me off my food. I stood aside and watched them eat while pretending to look as happy as them. I'd never been afraid of heights before but I was afraid to jump out of a plane. Eventually the Hercules aircraft lined up and taxied over to the various knots of soldiers waiting for their ride over to the drop zone. One Hercules stopped next to us and we ran on board just as we had been instructed.

The guys were singing. I didn't join in. I could hear huge

propeller engines, my friends singing and my own heartbeat, which drowned out the lot of them. The co-pilot of the plane was Liran's next-door neighbour and he stepped out of the cockpit with a camera. Everyone leaned in to smile and I put the best of British effort into offering what ended up as a kind of petrified movement on the side of my lips.

All too soon the jump lights clicked on near the doors at the rear of the plane. They looked like mini traffic lights but with only two lights instead of three. When amber came on we all stood up and faced the doors at the back. The aircraft were circling the drop zone and I knew my time was coming. The light turned green and I could vaguely see the first soldiers jumping as I shuffled forward for my turn. Then there was a scuffle at the front and a soldier sped past me towards the back of the plane. It was Omer, a soldier in the Sayeret. He was moving away from the open door but with nowhere to run he wasn't going to get far. Five instructors jumped on top of him, dragged him to the open door and threw him out. Now I knew I could rely on someone to kick me out if I froze at the door.

My turn came and I was standing at the door looking down on the sand dunes that constituted the drop zone far below. The jump instructor next to me was in his 50s and had a smile on his face. "Just put one hand on each side of the opening and don't look down!" he roared. So I looked down. The dunes of the beach were beneath me but the sea was far off. Dense clouds were above. The tips of my toes rested over the edge of the abyss. "Now push out just like you've been taught," he said. I pushed out. I was out of the aircraft screaming at the top of my lungs: "21, 22, 23 ..." I brought my knees up to my chest and kept my hands on my reserve parachute while I counted. With the three-second freefall over, I looked up to find, to my everlasting joy, that the parachute had deployed exactly as it was meant to.

The build-up had been a nightmare but the floating descent made it all worthwhile. I stared down past my dangling feet at the ground that was lazily coming closer, while marvelling at the fact that I had been given this opportunity by the army. I could hear others shouting to one another; some had brought their cameras with them and were busy taking pictures. All the fear and worry of the morning was exorcised by the ecstasy of drifting through the air with the aid of a parachute that had opened exactly as it was supposed to.

Soon, the ground was rushing up to meet me; we had been told that the fall after a parachute jump is equivalent to jumping from a height of 3m. I allowed my knees to buckle upon impact with the ground, just as they'd taught me. You'd think that after the first jump my worries about parachuting would have disappeared but they didn't. The fear grew greater before each jump. I hated everything up until the point the parachute opened. The floating through the air and the knowledge that I'd overcome my fear made the trip down a gift I could enjoy from start to finish.

The first jump had been without any equipment; on the second I jumped with a bag containing my infantry equipment strapped between my legs. Once the parachute deploys there's a lever on the parachute rig to pull that releases the bag, which is attached to the harness by a rope where it dangles until impact with the ground.

For the second time I shuffled to the door of the Hercules and jumped. One of the parachute cords twisted around my leg as the canopy deployed. I was suspended upside down. I started screaming at the parachute, "Give me my leg back!" I pulled on my leg and reached up with my arms to try and get a grip on the cord to release my foot. All the while the bag of equipment was pressing into my balls.

After tugging on the parachute cord and praying it wasn't going to break off, I freed my leg. The cord was all twisted and I had to kick out and spin around until the lines had untwisted. With that done my brain ordered my hand to pull the lever to release the bag from between my legs. But it was as if my hand had a mind all of its own.

"Are you sure that this lever does actually drop the bag down three metres?" hand asked brain.

"Yes I am, pull the lever," brain responded.

Hand still wasn't sure. "Are you sure pulling it won't simply see us fall out of the harness and to our deaths below?" hand enquired of brain.

"Yes, I'm sure, pull the lever," brain replied.

The argument between hand and brain continued until I pulled the lever and felt the reassuring drop of the bag from between my legs and the somewhat less reassuring tug on the rig as the cable went taut with the thing dangling beneath me. I then hit the ground, rolled, released the chute and jumped up ready to fight another day.

The next jump was a night jump and the jump after that another day jump. The fifth jump was cancelled due to bad weather. Four jumps were enough to qualify as an IDF parachutist. I had my silver wings and a ticket back to an evil pile of mud in the north of the West Bank.

17

GUARD DUTY

When I heard that we had guard duty coming up I was ecstatic. I figured it meant a break from the horrors of training. What I didn't know was that for 24 hours a day, every day, we would spend two hours guarding and two hours resting. Our officer then made that worse by insisting that it was forbidden to sleep between 10 a.m. and 10 p.m.

Advanced training wasn't all bad. After being in the army for three months we were allowed to call our officer by his name. He insisted on being called by his last, his surname, Black. At the time it was amazing. There was no more saluting either, not of Black, nor of anyone else. The Israeli army just wasn't an army in the European tradition. They hated saluting and they hated formality. I never learned how to march and I never had to iron a uniform or clean anything.

Day and night the area rang with the sound of small arms fire. It was eerie in the night to hear weapons popping constantly. When you're the one doing the shooting you notice the sounds of gunfire a lot less but standing in a guard post in the dark listening to it gave me a whole new perspective.

At first I liked guard duty. No one was fucking with me and there was usually someone else in a guard post so we could chat. Each two-hour shift finished quickly. There were no stretcher runs, or climbing up hills or mountains, and no assaulting dummy enemies at the top of a hill. After twenty-four hours of two hours on and two hours off, however, I started to feel the pressure. Soon I was counting every minute of my two hours off, weighing up every action according to how much sleep time I'd lose doing it. Should I waste five minutes brushing my teeth? Should I spend three minutes taking my uniform off or just sleep with it on? Should I spend one minute getting my boots off? Showering went out of the window almost straight away. There was no way I was giving up ten to fifteen minutes of sleep time to get clean only to stomp out of the showers into the mud and get dirty all over again. I waited as long as possible before going to the toilet.

After about three days I didn't know if I was awake or asleep at any given moment. Shifts of guard duty flew by leaving me unsure whether I'd been asleep on my feet or guarding. Other times guard duty seemed to last hours as I fought a mental battle to force my eyes to remain open.

The really interesting place to guard was the checkpoint on the road in front of the base. We'd open the road at 4 a.m., when it was still dark, and close it at around 8 p.m. The checkpoint consisted of a concrete barrier narrowing the road into a single lane and a position for one soldier to provide cover for another who would check the vehicles and question their occupants. Both soldiers outside were covered by more soldiers in bunkers at the entrance to the base giving them a view over the road. Next to guarding the checkpoint itself these were the two most interesting positions to be in; at least there was something going on outside.

It was while standing in one of the bunkers overlooking the road that I heard an explosion. I'd been watching the road trying to stay awake. It wasn't easy but I had developed a trick. I would look at a fixed object and tell myself about it. "Look at the rock, how would you describe it?" I asked myself. "Well, it's mossy and has plenty of stones around it, there are weeds around it too and it has a whitey grey colour." That wore thin after a while. At a certain point I would become aware that my eyes were closed and that I had moved from thinking about the rock to dreaming about it. I blinked my eyes back open again and tried to find something else to stare at.

This scenario played itself out during that shift until I heard the crash. I opened my eyes and climbed off the floor, rifle at the ready, and searched for the source of the explosion. The two soldiers were still on the road checking cars. Neither seemed to have heard anything. I turned and looked down at the ground I had just been lying on and understood. The sound of the explosion had been my helmeted head hitting the concrete floor. I had fallen asleep on my feet and collapsed. I drank some water and tried to focus on the road and covering the soldiers on it.

18

CHECKPOINT

The first time I manned the checkpoint I was backing up a squad leader who was doing the questioning. I covered him from behind a concrete block with a couple of sandbags on it. I was locked and loaded and aiming my weapon at real people for the first time. I peered at them through my marksman's scope ready to kill any of them: young men of military age, fat, middle-aged men, old women, young women, pregnant young women. I didn't know who was a threat and who wasn't. Was that bump a real pregnant belly or was it a bomb? Was the next car going to blow up when we stopped it? Questions paraded through my mind. There were no answers, only scenarios playing themselves out while I stood aiming my rifle at everyone who went past.

The routine was simple, cars lined up in both directions waiting for permission to pass. The squad leader moved from car to car, making checks. The Palestinians showed him their orange ID cards and he looked at them pretending that they meant something to him before waving them through. At four in the morning when we opened the checkpoint there was already a line of cars waiting to move and when we closed it at night the road was deserted.

Many of the cars were beaten-up pieces of rust and metal filled to bursting. Once I inspected the boot of a vehicle to find seven sheep stuffed inside while the moustachioed owner of the car stood awkwardly by. There were minibuses and regular buses, old cars and even the odd horse and cart moving through our checkpoint. This was the first time I had met any Palestinians and I pointed my rifle at every one of them. Most of the time I saw them through the cross hairs of my scope while I waited for one of them to make a move and earn one of my bullets. But no one did.

19

THE BREAKING OF A SOLDIER

Kfir was the biggest, strongest member of the team. He was the machine gunner and he could lift anything. No pack was too heavy on his back and no distance was too great. He breezed through the gibush and he finished basic training without breaking a sweat. He was one of the main guys in the tzevet and the two of us had the midnight to 2 a.m. shift in the bunkers overlooking the road.

At that time of night the checkpoint was closed. The rain blew into our bunkers and the chill left us both shivering. There was no way of getting out of the weather and the two of us, separately, had to stand in our positions and suffer through it while waiting for our relief to come and switch us over. The relief never came. Five minutes passed and then ten minutes, which became twenty and then thirty. The only thing on our minds was our sleep time. We couldn't abandon our positions to find out what was going on and there was no one on the end of the radio.

Eventually my relief arrived in the form of a soaking wet member of the Sayeret. "Sorry, man, but it's the storm. All the tents have been blown down!" he said. I didn't believe him; I figured they had overslept.

On the way back Kfir said, "If the tents have blown down I'm going to sleep in the toilets."

"Yeah me too!" I jokingly agreed as we sloshed through the mud back to our encampment.

All the tents had collapsed in the storm, just as we'd been told. My thoughts jumped to my bag of once dry clothes now underneath a big square of canvas with water running through it. I ran to our tent and worked with the others to get it back up. To make sure the tent stayed up we needed to fill sand bags with dirt and figure out a way to tie enough of them to the bottom of the tent to make sure none of the pegs would be tugged out by the strength of the wind.

We got to work shovelling dirt while Elad went under the canvas to lift up the two central beams that were supposed to hold the tent upright. We worked together and when the beams were up I knew that we were on our way to winning a small victory against nature … but where was Kfir?

Someone voiced the question and for a moment we all stopped and looked around. In all the commotion I had forgotten about him but I knew where he was. Several of the guys followed me to the bathroom where we found him fast asleep on a bench. Most of the guys were still outside working while he lay there refusing to move. We shouted at him, tugged him, kicked him and tried everything we could to get him up but he wouldn't budge … he was finished. Not just for the night but for everything to do with the tzevet.

He had walked away when we had needed him the most. Kfir had been a core member from the beginning but just like that he was nothing. None of us had ever actually spoken about the rules of the group but they were crystal clear, and rule number one was that you don't abandon your friends. Kfir committed the greatest sin a soldier in training could commit and without even speaking of it to each other we all abandoned him. No one wanted to be seen with him, to sit next to him, to talk to him. Eventually he was kicked out by Black, but it was right there in those filthy toilets during that storm that he had made the decision that this wasn't for him. And we in turn decided he wasn't for us.

20

WEEKEND: MIKE'S PLACE

I sat there drinking my way into the oblivion that only large quantities of alcohol can provide. I don't remember most of that evening but I can remember the end vividly. The barman was getting annoyed with me because every time I picked up my glass I spilled some beer onto the counter and he had to wipe it up. I looked around and saw that somehow what had been a bar filled with revellers had become empty and that the shutters were halfway down. The evening was over and most people were already home in bed. I looked back at the barman who said to me, "The others said I should throw you out, but I said so long as your money is good you can stay." He shrugged and walked to the other side of the bar. I had what many drunks refer to as "a moment of clarity": it was time to leave.

I didn't get far. I woke up a few hours later about 10m away from the pub. The sand of the beach had been my bed. The sun was beating down on me as I patted my pockets to make sure I hadn't been robbed while I slept. I hadn't. I crawled into the shade where I promptly passed out again. When I awoke I made my way home to shower away the sand, before getting into a real bed and nursing my hangover. At some point I got a call from Dave. He had moved to Israel from London at the same time as me; we had met on the Ulpan in Jerusalem. We had abandoned that city for Tel Aviv at about the same time and he now worked as a barman at Mike's Place. When he told me to come over for lunch I couldn't think of a reason not to, so back I went.

Walking in there I felt like I was revisiting the scene of a crime but I managed to get over it enough to nod hello to Dave as I sat across from him and ordered a Coke. He grinned in a way that loudly announced: "I know why you're not ordering a beer." He then said, "Sure you don't want a beer?"

I smiled and shook my head, "No thanks mate, just the Coke." The only other customers were sitting at one of the tables enjoying some time in the shade; with no one else there and nothing for him to do we bantered a little bit, there was a waitress there too and she joined in the conversation. She was French, she was tall and had very closely cropped hair. Mike's Place always seemed to attract people like us. Foreigners looking for something familiar – people speaking English, sport from our home countries, or maybe just companionship with people who knew what we meant when we would talk about where we were from.

The walls were plastered with Americana and old adverts for Coke. There was a jukebox, a pool table and loads of televisions showing the most popular British and American sports games, and when there wasn't a game it would be the extreme sports channel. At night you would always hear a cacophony of different accents in there all trying to speak English over the noise of whatever rock music was being played LOUD. During the day, though, it was different story; the tourists who filled the bar in the evening were too busy sunning themselves on the beach to worry about getting a cheeseburger.

So the three of us sat there. I ordered a burger and listened to Dave tell me the story about his latest conquest, the ease with which a barman could get women and how much all the bosses loved him. The waitress smiled politely, I ate slowly, the music played loudly and the sun beat down outside. We carried on talking shit until one of the bosses walked in. He nodded hello to us before going into the office. Dave promptly found stuff to clean and the waitress did a round of the other customers sitting there to make sure they were okay.

I had brought with me a map that had been distributed to

us before we left for the weekend so that we would be up to speed for the next week of navigation training. When the boss came out of the office and saw me studying it he sat with me. Everyone there already whispered about his military service, about how he dropped just enough hints to let you know he was in some ultra-cool combat unit but then never actually spoke about it. He went over with me how to recognise the direction that water flows in simply by looking at the map. He showed me how the various small rivers all form little arrows into the bigger rivers that they run into. These arrows on the map point out the direction the water flows. When I started asking him where he served in the army he wandered off.

At the bar Dave offered me a free brownie from a dish near him. He and the waitress watched as I took a bite and swallowed it, "Dominique made them," he said with a nod towards the tall waitress watching me eat, waiting to hear what I thought of her cooking. I didn't like it but I think I convinced her it tasted great.

The TV was on in the background. CNN showed American Humvees ploughing into Iraq. I still had four months of training to get through before I would be going out on operations. I tried not to think about the fact that once again I didn't want to go back in. The feeling reminded me of a kid I saw walk out of the gibush during a rest period. There was nothing tough going on, no reason for him to choose to quit at that moment. We were nearer the end with each second that passed and yet he chose to walk away. I now understood him. During training there wasn't much time to think about quitting, or about whether I was happy or whether the army was meeting my expectations, but when I was home, left to my own devices, that was when thoughts of quitting came into my head. The control someone had over every aspect of my life was exposed in all its horror when those limitations were suddenly removed. I thought of England, of my friends. I felt utterly alone in this distant land, despite being surrounded by people all the time.

I remember calling a friend in London that evening and staying on the phone to him while I walked to a cafe and sat there and ate an entire meal. Loneliness had set in. The relief of being able to talk to someone in English, without having to aimlessly grapple for words outside my vocabulary, was incredibly important. I didn't care what we spoke about, I just wanted to hear a voice from home.

The next morning I was on a bus to the north. Uniforms cleaned and rifle in hand for more navigation training. At the end of one night's trekking with the sun already up Uzi and I arrived back to camp. One of the camp's medics was on guard duty and waved us in.

"Did you hear?" he asked. "Mike's Place was blown up tonight, don't know how many dead." Then he flicked his cigarette into the morning, got up and went off to sleep.

It turned out I wasn't the only British volunteer in the Holy Land. There were at least two others. Both of them wore suicide vests but only one of them found paradise immediately. He took three people with him, one of whom was Dominique, the French girl with the cropped hair who had given me one of her brownies.

It was the first time the conflict had really pierced the all-embracing canopy of the army. I was so involved in training that the events in the outside world barely registered. As a trainee soldier I was a baby in the womb, still being grown, still being prepared for the outside war. That bomb sent a shock wave that I could feel even through the protection afforded to me by the army. I hadn't known Dominique well but I had known her none the less. She was the first person whose life had been taken by this conflict to be more than a statistic to me. I had spoken to her, I had seen her smile, seen her work and joke and laugh. I had felt the touch of her presence and now she was no more, never to make more brownies, never to grace the bar again, never to feel the touch of old age, to have children, or enjoy the opportunities offered by this world.

It was difficult to know what to think or how to feel. The fact that the bombers were also British made me feel as though they had pulled away the last vestiges of my British identity. I was Israeli now and I was in the army of my people, prepared to give my life to protect them. The fact that these two men had shared the same country with me for most of our lives made me feel much more convinced that I was in the right place doing the right thing.

I was here to defend the people they had come to kill.

21

RED BERET

I remember every step I took over the 23 hours it took to complete the 90km march for my red beret. We began near the town of Rehovot by the Mediterranean and finished at Ammunition Hill, the site of the Paratrooper's victory over the Jordanian army in 1967. At the start we moved through soft, almost marshy ground that my red paratrooper boots sank into. I remember thinking that if the ground remained that way until we reached Jerusalem I was never going to make it.

We marched through the height of the day to sunset and into the night. We started in high spirits, happy that it would all soon be over, chatting as we marched. After a while we were alone in our own special mental world, that place we had constructed where we could concentrate on forcing our bodies upwards to Jerusalem.

During one of the breaks one of the guys threw the radio down onto the ground. He'd had enough. Without thinking I picked it up and put it on my back. To my surprise it fitted snugly, as if it was made for me. I remained at the front of the team from the moment I took it conveying messages to the officer and relishing the fact that the days of extreme pain were way behind me.

When the ground became steeper I knew we were climbing the slopes up to Jerusalem. The seat of King David's power. I was walking over soil fertilised by the blood of the Jewish warriors who had gone before me. I was climbing to the end of the torture of training and the attainment of my greatest aspiration in life.

My parents had come to see me gain my red beret. I recalled that moment in Manchester when I watched those girls leaving the recruitment fair. Another world, another dimension. A reality devoid of stretcher marches, rifles and green uniforms. It was a dimension devoid of tents that blew down in the rain, of soldiers struggling, of officers giving orders seemingly impossible to carry out until they were proved possible by sweat and teamwork. It was a world that belonged to a different me, to a boy looking for a home, looking for a purpose and a direction in life. I wondered if my parents would recognise me. I wondered if I would recognise myself. I wondered these things while ascending to Jerusalem.

And then we weren't moving cross-country any more, we were marching close to roads and underpasses, bridges and civilisation. We stopped. The captain looked back at us. "Open the stretchers," he shouted. We knew what was coming. We, the newest Paratroopers, were to run up to Ammunition Hill in our final rite of passage.

We stood, stretchers on our shoulders, tense, like catapults waiting to be released. The captain stared at us blankly as if he didn't care, the same way the other commanders had looked at us from the beginning, as if we were nothing, like we had no idea what we had got ourselves into, like he detested our mere presence. In our final moment of glory I saw nothing in his face expressing the feeling of elation that we all shared. I saw only pain and worry, a look that warned that this moment lacked all meaning, rhyme and reason. I hated him for it.

"GO!" he shouted and as one we ran. I can't remember who was on the stretcher or who was around me, I just remember sprinting forward down a road. I remember the motorists hooting their horns as they saw us pass, some with their fists in the air. I remember seeing people smiling, I remember not being able to keep up with the stretcher no matter how hard I tried. I ran until I could hardly breathe and until I couldn't tell the difference between the sweat dripping from my forehead and the tears spilling from my eyes. It was over at the end of the road. It was over when I reached the place where my Paratrooper forebears had broken open the road to Jerusalem. It ended at Ammunition Hill.

22

A Paratrooper is Born

We couldn't stop hugging each other. We couldn't stop smiling and laughing and loving the fact that we had made it. Ammunition Hill marked the Paratrooper victory in 1967 but now it was the place where Marc Goldberg, serial number 5489872, earned his red beret. It wasn't just a battlefield any more; it was the place where my dream came true.

We drank the chocolate milk, and ate the cheese and yoghurt and everything else that had been laid on for us. When the excitement subsided we felt the sores that come from moving for so long in full kit and it wasn't long before none of us could move without feeling the pain in our bodies. But it didn't matter. We had done it!

The music was played over the PA system and after being ordered to stand to attention and then to stand at ease several times our names were called. My officer was standing next to a table with crimson berets laid out in neat lines. If I had looked closer I would have noticed that a watch was sitting there also.

When my turn came I stepped forward but instead of moving to the table to grab my beret and place it on my head my officer stepped back grinning and the squad leader stepped forward. He took his own beret off his head and placed it on mine, then Black presented me with the watch sitting on the table. "You were the best on the march," he said. I felt my face redden. I had only ever tried to get through the training not be the best at anything. But there, in front of my comrades and my family I was being rewarded not with a flat, shapeless beret but with the battered beret of my commander, a sign of respect for my personal achievement, a sign of excellence.

When it was all done we threw our berets into the air and jumped up and down before running to find our families. Mine found me and I was being embraced by my parents and my brothers all at once. What a strange journey I had dragged them on, from going on holidays to Miami, Florida and Spain when we were growing up to the site of a battle they had never heard of in a country they knew only vaguely at best. They shared in my dream and took pride in my success. They hugged me after having watched me win the beret of my commander and a watch from my officer. They were there because of me and I was there to achieve my dream. I knew that my dream was never theirs and yet there we all were on Ammunition Hill.

All the families there had brought food from home for their sons; my family brought me sushi from the Tel Aviv Hilton. The day after the march I was with my brothers somewhere in the bowels of the Hilton while my Mum was in the room. The maid entered to clean up. She saw my uniform thrown on the floor then looked at my mother and, in a heavy Russian accent, she asked about the uniform. My mother explained that her oldest son was in Israel serving, "Your son in the army is the son of all of us," she said.

My mother cried.

23

FIRST MISSION

We were to creep into the city during the night, occupy strategic locations and kill any terrorists who showed their faces. Each tzevet in the unit was given two locations to take over ensuring that my tzevet would be split into two squads. We looked at some maps, plotted the routes into the city and then each of us went off to get ready for our first experience of the real thing.

There were vehicles all around us. We stood in our full battle kit, locked, loaded and ready for war. My face was smeared with black, grey and brown camouflage cream and thoughts of death flowed through my mind as I pondered the meaning of the unit commander, Cobi's parting words, "We have an excellent chance for kills tonight".

Would I kill someone tonight? Was I to join the ranks of the initiated? This was a combat mission in the legendary Nablus – city of the suicide bombers. Anticipation was mixed with a tiny bit of dread. Perhaps the only thing waiting for me in Nablus was a bullet in the brain. Perhaps I wouldn't save Israel on that night or any other. Perhaps all I was doing was stepping out into an evil night inhabited by men who wanted nothing more than the honour of killing me, an Israeli soldier.

We were travelling in a vehicle called a "Knight", an armoured car I was entirely unfamiliar with. Up to ten of us squeezed into an area designed for about six. There were two tiny, metal benches facing one another in the rear of the Knight. In between them the team would insert themselves any way they could. In full kit it was a problem but somehow we always managed it. Later in my service it would become such a routine operation that I would even fall asleep on the ride in – but not that night.

And then we were in Nablus. Driving through the streets of the city all I could make out was the light beaming down from the lamp posts. Soon enough we came to a stop, the instruction "prika" (out) came from Black up front. This was it. I kicked at the unfamiliar doors; they opened to the sudden burst of force and we all bounded out into a summer night in Nablus.

The vehicles dropped us off at the outskirts of the city to prevent the noise of their engines alerting any terrorists to our approach. Standing there among the low buildings on an asphalt road I felt I could have been in any city. There was nothing about Nablus, with her lamp posts and neat homes, that made me feel as if my life was in danger.

I took my place in the formation in the centre of the squad of 9. We were all there together, waiting in formation, when word came to move. At first, I walked as if taking my first steps on the moon, expecting at any moment I would simply float away. I wondered if I had it all wrong, whether this was really happening. Was I really among a bunch of Israeli commandos in the middle of an Arab city? Was I really carrying a weapon capable of inflicting tremendous pain and death?

As one long snake we wound our way through Nablus from that pleasant suburb towards the city centre. We didn't walk; we crept, feet kissing the ground while inching forward, ears straining for any sound out of the ordinary. Our eyes became attuned to the artificial light of the lamp posts and searched the shadows, attempting to spot anyone waiting within them. We did this as we moved towards our goal in the kasbah, the ancient heart of the city.

The night felt like an enemy hiding other enemies behind a veil through which my eyes couldn't see. What had been small buildings became ever taller and more closely packed together until I couldn't tell where one ended and another began. The walls were filled with Arabic scrawls and posters. There were thousands of posters of suicide bombers complete with pictures taken from television reports of the carnage they had caused. They covered every available space, save for the occasional poster of Arafat looking up with an angelic light falling on his face.

Someone kicked a can of Coke, sending it sliding through the night, destroying the protection of silence. We sank down to one knee, weapons raised, looking to see if the intrusion of sound into silence had awoken any beasts of the night. I glanced up. I looked at all the windows of homes directly above me and to the side of me. Lights came from some; others were in darkness. A single grenade dropped from a window would have decimated us.

Nothing happened. The noise disappeared into the recesses of the stone streets and alleyways. We rose and continued towards the kasbah, the heart of Nablus. Upon arrival in the dank centre, two squads peeled away on their own journey towards their target. Watching them move silently through the concentrated urban centre gave me a feeling of power. I was one of them now.

Black led us into one of the many alleys that appeared throughout the centre of the city. I wasn't sure whether it was a relief to be in a dark place or more frightening to be in such a confined space. I had savoured the taste of moving around in the city up to that point. I was in enemy territory and I had been working for a full year for the right to be there. Now I was in Nablus, whose very stones seemed to scream at me: "You are not wanted here, get out, get out now." For all the tension the city was so quiet. There was no movement and there were no people. Was this the dangerous city I had heard so much about? I couldn't help but ask myself. I remembered all those war films where the hero utters the cliché, "it's too quiet".

After crouching for 30 seconds or so we rose and moved forward. If there was anyone awake in the buildings we passed they could easily have called the relevant people and alerted them to our presence. Occasionally a light went on in a room above us or hushed tones could be heard coming from an open window. Someone would point their weapon in the general direction and we would move on.

When we arrived at our first target – an empty office building – our sergeant took his squad and entered while the rest of us remained outside. Once the sergeant radioed that the building was 'clean' my squad continued to our own target. We took a right turn down a narrow alleyway where garbage was piled high. My boots disappeared up to my ankle in filth. Here we stopped. I was at the rear watching the main road. An elderly Palestinian man, hunched over and using a walking stick was plodding up the road towards us. Our entry was supposed to be covert. My orders at the start were that I could open fire on anyone breaking curfew, but he was just an old man. He came closer and I nudged the soldier next to me (a kibbutznik with four months more experience than me).

"Did he see you?" he whispered.

"No," I replied.

We both held our breath as he walked past our alleyway without looking in our direction.

We continued on our journey. There were more posters on the walls celebrating suicide bombers. They were all the same – with the face of the bomber and the name of the terrorist group claiming responsibility for an attack, all scrawled in Arabic. A filmstrip running along the bottom portrayed the carnage he or she had caused and told of the number of dead and wounded. Later, I would collect the posters as souvenirs. For the moment, though, I was awestruck as the faces of Palestinian "martyrs" looked down on me.

We reached our objective: a block of flats. We went in and found ourselves in a stairwell. I expected a grenade to be tossed down at any second. My squad waited just inside the opening to the building while Black took his three men to the top floor to clean out the two apartments located there. When this was complete he radioed down to us and we moved up the three flights of stairs to join him.

Adrenaline rushed through me in waves. I thought back to training exercises we had undergone in a crumbling British fort. Firing and covering and manoeuvring, then doing it all over again. This was a big block. If there was opposition inside it would have needed a company to pacify it but we were just a few first-timers. Moving through the silent building, I looked at the doors to people's homes, wondering what mysteries lay behind them. Where was the guy with the gun out to get me? Where was the martyr, already dead in spirit, waiting only for the opportunity to die in a blast of fire and shrapnel? Were they here? Were they waiting for me? Don't forget to look up, don't forget to cover your angles I reminded myself. Nothing happened and we reached the top in a massive burst of anticlimax.

Black was awaiting our arrival and directed us into one of the two apartments. I stepped through the front door into a living room. The top halves of the walls were painted white and the lower halves grey. There was a kitchen in a further room to my left. Directly opposite the front door there was a sliding door, with small square windows set into the wood. A slight man with shoulder-length hair sat on an old couch in the living room. He was smoking a cigarette and holding an ashtray in his quivering hands. He kept flicking the ash, almost extinguishing the cigarette. His eyes made contact with mine then darted away. Next to him sat his wife, a plump woman who spoke good English, which she later told me she learned at Birzeit University. Alongside her sat an old woman dressed in white robes and wearing a headscarf. The two women were talking animatedly in hushed tones.

Black followed us into the room. There were two small children sleeping in the room next door and he saw no reason to wake them he told us casually. The word "children" caught me off guard. I glanced back at the door with two sleeping toddlers beyond. He explained that he would be staying in another apartment with four soldiers who would take turns on a sniper position they had created there. The rest of us would be staying in this other apartment looking after the civilians.

I felt like I'd been punched. That was it? All the tension, all the adrenaline and feelings of fear and excitement crashed. My role was to stay in the apartment as an unpaid babysitter. My fears about becoming a changed man, about being in danger, about having to pull the trigger for the first time against a living target were for nothing. I felt embarrassed even to have been concerned.

Naturally these thoughts remained unspoken. There was nothing to say and the others were probably thinking the same as me anyway. The fact that my irritation remained tacit did not mean that it went away. We divided guard duty between us and I came up second. We would do two hours each, which meant six hours between each shift. We went to sleep in the master bedroom after the family had taken the blankets and pillows they would need. Orders with regards to sleeping were simple: no using any of the family's furniture, no taking off of the bullet proof vests and no removing boots. I lied down on the floor and fell asleep immediately.

When my turn came to take watch I was roused by Natan, our medic, who had taken the first shift. He gave me the radio and told me where to sit. The door had been left slightly ajar and a chair positioned to allow me to see if anyone was coming up the stairs. All the family were asleep under a load of blankets and pillows. The radio kept making strange noises. All the different teams from my unit were reporting in. Unfortunately for me, I couldn't understand anything they were saying. I continued listening, becoming more and more anxious as I realised the responsibility I held in my hands. Eventually, I plucked up the courage to report in. I received no response. Sod it, I thought, at least I tried. After an hour and forty-five minutes I left my post to wake up Uzi who took over.

It felt as though I was being shaken awake the second after I closed my eyes. My squad commander was tapping my shoulder. Light was streaming into the room so I guessed I had been sleeping for at least a couple of hours. He woke me with the words, "The British are here". I rose slightly. My bulletproof vest made sitting upright a struggle and I gave him my arm to help me up. Certain my bad Hebrew and fatigue were distorting my hearing, I entered the main room of the apartment to find – to my horror – that we had gone from having five guests, including the two children, to an entire clan squeezed in.

There were the couple's cousins and their two children as well as the old woman's nephew and his wife who had decided to come around out of concern for their aunt. A pregnant lady friend of the plump wife had decided to "pop in" and hadn't stopped crying since. As if this weren't enough, there were four foreign volunteers (Peacemakers in IDF vernacular), two American and two British. I had come to destroy Hamas in my first operation; they had come to end the plight of the Palestinian people in a two-week visit.

One of the British peacemakers was a tall, dark-haired, Oxford undergraduate, who was volunteering during his summer break. There was another guy – a gaunt, blond American who didn't say much, other than to repeatedly mutter under his breath, "This situation would be a whole lot better if everyone would just smoke a joint." There were also two girls, both of whom were around 19 or 20. The American girl was short with dimples and seemed to me to have come straight out of a film. She was constantly demanding in her high-pitched, whiny voice to be allowed to call the American consulate. I wasn't sure how she thought the consulate could possibly help her. The other girl was tall and thin, with deep, dark eyes; boasting a London accent she reminded me of the Asian girls from home. I felt comfortable around her. Which was weird.

And so began my second turn at guard duty. There I stood,

all five feet six inches of me, alone in the room wearing a bullet proof ceramic plate covered by a combat vest bristling with ammunition and grenades, as well as, of course, my beautiful M4 flat top rifle complete with X4 amplification scope and no enemies to train it on.

No one in the team spoke any English except for me, especially not Black who barely understood yes and no. So, even with my dodgy Hebrew, I became the translator of the group, sending messages back and forth between my officer and our new captives. They didn't understand why we were holding them. I explained that, were we to let them go everyone outside would know we were holed up in the apartment. They stared back at me before the English girl said, "They all know already. Why do you think they asked us to come here and check on the people you're holding? They said you would never keep 'us' in here against our will!" She emphasised the word us.

Her answer was disconcerting. Our supposedly covert entry had been anything but. To make matters worse, instead of being met by a welcoming committee of masked gunmen, we were met by four peacemakers from the USA and UK. I would have preferred the gunmen. I had been trained to take on gunmen but I didn't even know that volunteers were a "thing" in the West Bank. I asked Black if we could just let them go but he was adamant. "No one can leave!"

So there we all were stuck together in the apartment. The temperature rose throughout the day. It was mid-August and the heat was sweltering. I felt sweat seeping through my uniform. The four peacemakers were sitting together on a seat opposite everyone else who was sitting on the old couches in the living room. To talk to one group I had to turn from the other.

"Aren't you hot in all that stuff?" inquired the British girl sweetly. Was she mocking me?

"Oh no, I'm used to it," I said as nonchalantly as I could.

"Don't you ever feel disgusted that you do all this?" asked the British kid.

I laughed in genuine surprise. I had come a long way to defend my people, I had passed through tougher training than I had imagined possible to arrive precisely at this moment and arrest or kill terrorists attempting to blow up innocent civilians.

"No." I said a smile still on my face. "There are people out there who wish to do a great deal of harm to innocent people in Israel. I would rather stop them here in their own city than run the risk of them arriving in Tel Aviv." And so began a five-hour debate about the Israeli–Palestinian conflict, punctuated at times by sirens and the sound of faraway gunshots. We were also interrupted by an American accent shrieking: "Now I really am going to call the embassy!" every now and then.

We discussed the supply of water:

"You know that the Israeli government severely restricts the amount of water that Palestinians can have, don't you?" he spat at me.

"You know that there is no water in the Middle East, don't you?" I spat back. "In 1967 we fought a war and won. Had we lost, this argument would be irrelevant, as my people would have been expelled from the Middle East! Murdered, dead, finished and no one would fucking care!" After I said that it went quiet. I looked around. All the civilians were sitting forward looking at me. As one they all seemed to lean back into their seats.

He either became quiet because I had won or because I had become angry. I am not sure which. The argument didn't end there and we continued only to be interrupted now and again by an American accented voice saying: "I'm calling the consulate!" But she didn't. And so I began again with the British kid, arguing about everything from the devastation caused by Israeli bulldozers knocking down the homes of suicide bombers, to the amount of time it would take the Palestinians to rebuild their cities in the wake of Operation Defensive Shield. My time on guard came and went and still we argued. When Uzi came to replace me I told him not to bother.

In the middle, the woman whose flat I had taken over let loose an impassioned plea, the plea of civilians caught in a war zone all around the world: "We are not terrorists, we are normal people trying to live our lives. Why have you come here"?

Her appeal would not move me: "The army needs your apartment. Were there no terrorists blowing themselves up there would be no army presence here at all".

The British kid told me that the clinic for which this woman was responsible couldn't open because we were holding her captive. It seemed ridiculous. We were here in Nablus preventing suicide bombers leaving the city to get to their targets. "If a handful of people couldn't get to a clinic today, then they'll go tomorrow," I said. Inside though, he had given me pause for thought. I couldn't be sure that what I was doing was contributing to stopping bombers. I was simply holed up in the apartment. Was anything I was doing actually helping?

"The only reason there are terrorists is because you are here!" the British kid said to me.

"No," I corrected him. "The only reason we're here is because there are terrorists!" I surveyed the room and noticed that my captives were once again sitting forward attempting to understand this argument between the British-born Israeli soldier and the Oxford undergraduate peacemaker.

I stopped, afraid I had said too much. They were used to the sirens and gunshots that provided a constant backdrop of noise. An insight into the mind of an Israeli soldier was something new. I didn't mind them listening in because I wanted them to understand me. We aren't murderers; we don't do this simply to ruin your lives. We have no choice but to stop the bombers. Yet still I was scared I had said too much. My job was to guard them not to talk to them.

As we finished our argument a murmur went through the

group and the pregnant woman started crying. She had been crying for most of the time that I had been in the room. I told the plump woman who spoke English to tell her not to worry, that we would be gone soon. My comment was met with a shrill, American-accented "She can cry if she wants to!" from the American girl. I looked at her but I had nothing to say. Anyway, Uzi came back to relieve me, something for which, at that moment, I was profoundly grateful.

I went into the master bedroom to find the guys making a feast of the bread rolls and tinned tuna we had brought with us. Not feeling particularly hungry, but looking for comfort, I sat down with my friends and helped myself. As per usual there was not enough ketchup and I had to make do with mustard.

Once eating was over I sparked up a cigarette and watched the blue grey smoke curl up towards the ceiling. There were sirens going off outside again. I wished I was there 'taking care of business'. Instead I was stuck in a flat with a bunch of whiny tourists and some Palestinian civilians, not to mention kids.

It was late when I went back on guard; soon it would be dark. I scanned the room. There were still a lot of people in it and I was on my own. What if one of them tried to escape? Would I shoot? How could I ever justify killing a civilian trying to escape from his own house? So I decided I wouldn't shoot, but I wouldn't let someone get away either. If it came to it I would use the butt of my rifle to down my enemy. I noticed I had my weapon clipped to me rather than on a sling and that I would never have been able to use the butt to hit anyone. So I surreptitiously went about the process of unclipping the weapon and attaching the strap. As I did this I realised that it would make it easier for someone to remove the weapon from me. Then I remembered that was the reason I had clipped the rifle to me in the first place. What if they all decided to rush me? There were a lot of them and if they all moved together they could get my weapon. Would I kill civilians then? I was tired. It was a stupid argument to be having with myself. We were in an apartment filled with soldiers – if anything happened they would have taken care of it in the blink of an eye.

It had become more than obvious to all of us in the apartment that everyone outside knew we were there. The Red Crescent had been shouting up to us for permission to bring in medical supplies. With the news Black made one of his infrequent forays in to 'our' apartment as opposed to the one with the all-important sniper position. He surveyed the situation and saw the pregnant woman who was still crying. I asked him if we could get her out of there now that it was obvious that people outside were aware of us. He promised to radio the higher ups and see what he could do. In addition to this, the British girl was talking about how she needed her medication for a high blood pressure and could she ask the Red Crescent guys to get it for her. This was all a little too much and once again I found myself wishing for some armed enemy to appear so that I could involve myself in a firefight rather than having to deal with the trials and tribulations of babysitting.

The American girl decided to come out of the toilet and complain that someone had not flushed it. "Probably one of the soldiers," she said. "I bet they don't even know how to use Palestinian bathrooms," she said with a pointed look at me. Even in a room in a foreign country, surrounded by men with guns holding her captive, she still found it within herself to be condescending. What annoyed me even more was that I had been the last person to use the toilet and, no, I did not know how to flush a Palestinian toilet.

It was at this point that the chubby woman, whose flat we were in, decided to ask me when we were going to leave. Of course I didn't have a clue, and even if I had known, I probably wouldn't have been able to tell her. But I didn't want it to be obvious that this was my first mission so I told her to be patient in as confident and authoritative a voice as I could muster. Just after I said it she stage whispered to the British girl, "He doesn't know," and they both giggled. I sighed, standing there with camouflage cream on my face in the middle of an apartment being mocked by my own captives without a terrorist in sight. I wondered if I was the only soldier who managed to get ridiculed by his own captives.

"I think they will leave tonight when it gets dark," she said, "That's what they always do." That's what we always do? I almost asked her what time we usually leave. Instead I glanced at my watch – five o'clock – not long until darkness. I hoped the lady was right.

Soon enough Black dragged himself away from the sniper position to come into our apartment and let the pregnant woman go. Her tears of anguish turned to tears of joy. I returned to the master bedroom for another smoke and some sleep. While I was sleeping Black let everyone else go. Strangely enough, I felt a little annoyed that I hadn't been around to say goodbye to them, especially the girl. I guessed now they had a story to tell of their experience at the hands of the evil IDF. I felt sure that by the time their plane touched the ground in the USA or UK their story would have transformed into soldiers holding them hostage as human shields and beating them mercilessly.

We picked up the paraphernalia of our short stay – the wrappers, cigarette butts and assorted waste, and stuffed it into the rucksack Uzi had carried in with him on his back. Once finished, we vacated the bedroom and Black gave the family leave to roam freely. Immediately the lady attacked the floor of her bedroom with a mop and bucket. I felt bad watching her work. Even though we had tried to clear up there was still ash and the crumbs of the meals we had eaten there. Within a couple of minutes there was no evidence we'd ever been there at all.

The man of the house started talking for the first time. He explained he used to work in Israel as a builder during Oslo. Since our arrival the kids had been quiet; now they were running around the apartment. With the news of our imminent departure and the release of the people trapped in the apartment a dark cloud lifted from all of us. Uzi learnt from the father that one of the kids knew a popular Israeli song so we all sat listening to him sing it to us. We all patted him on the back and complimented the man on having a son with such a voice. I wondered where on earth planet Nablus was located and whether it was an armoured car or a space ship that had brought me there.

Black's guys followed him in to our apartment and we swapped stories about what we had been doing for the past day or so. It turned out that Forrest thought he had caught a glimpse of an armed man on the street. I was jealous. And then it was time to leave. We said our goodbyes to the family and told them we hoped they wouldn't be bothered again. We hoisted packs onto our backs, checked weapons, did a final sweep of the flat to make sure nothing had been left behind and then followed Black out of the door and down the stairs. It felt good to be outside. The summer air came with the stench of garbage from the alley we had crouched in the night before but at least I was moving and in the open air.

We moved back to the empty building we had left the sergeant and his team in the night before. The guys there had had an uneventful time. The unoccupied building ensured they hadn't had to cater to any civilians. At first I was jealous of the fact that they hadn't been burdened by peacemakers and crying pregnant women. Later on I decided that there couldn't have been a better introduction to operational life than this claustrophobic experience. I wasn't sure what I had learnt in those 24 hours. Perhaps it was simply that Palestinians are people too, with their own hopes, dreams and aspirations for the future and that those don't always involve killing Jews.

I watched more and more soldiers file into the building. Sweat had wiped away the camouflage cream from our faces and what was left behind simply looked as though a little muck had been thrown on here and there. Sentries were posted and the more experienced guys fell straight to sleep. They knew that simply because we had all met up it didn't necessarily mean we were leaving. They valued sleep as others value gold and took the opportunity to get as much of it as possible. I just sat there like the inexperienced trooper I was, wondering what the hold up could be. Why were we just sitting there? Surely no one had forgotten about us. Later I would learn that these questions are irrelevant. The lowly soldier doesn't have the luxury of asking why, or how, or when. You go where they send you, you sit where they tell you to and what happens happens.

Eventually word came through that we were leaving. Soldiers were roused from their state of semi-sleep and organised back into their respective squads. The walk back to the jumping-off point was every bit as exhilarating as the walk from it and every bit as uneventful. We walked past the sinister alleyways and the stones that were now smiling at my departure. Past the posters of suicide bombers all under the bright, white Palestinian lamp posts. Once in the armoured car I tried to reflect upon what I had been through. Hamas hadn't been destroyed and it appeared they wouldn't be any time soon. I hoped we wouldn't have to deal with civilians any more. I still hadn't learnt that fighting terrorists always involves dealing with civilians. The terrorists themselves are civilians right up to the point at which they blow themselves up. Finally the rhythm of the vehicle got to me and I was able to close my eyes and leave my thoughts behind as the dark veil of sleep fell upon me.

24

THE SMILER

Qalqilya is a city in the West Bank that sits almost on the Green Line separating Israeli sovereign territory from Israeli occupied territory. It's about ten miles from the Mediterranean coast and is at the narrowest point of Israel's slim waistline. It's where I was to be riding shotgun in a vehicle tasked with picking up a team of our troops who had been in the city conducting an ambush overnight.

That's how I came to be sitting with a bunch of combat engineers watching a VHS of Pretty Woman. It was one of only five movies they had. The tapes had degraded to almost nothing and we watched the film with fuzzy lines all over the screen. Boaz would be driving. He finished his training four months before me, liked talking in stupid voices, positively rippled with muscles and always seemed to be at the doctor's. All I had to do was sit next to him in the car.

Everyone knew Qalqilya wasn't really a terrorist hotspot so operating there was kind of looked down on. Boaz seemed to know the way there, which was good because I hadn't a clue. Soon enough we hit the outskirts of the city. First it was just the odd house on the side of the road but then more appeared. It was about 10 in the morning when we drove in and there were more than a few people about. The area around us moved from rural to urban awfully quickly. I gazed out of the bulletproof glass at the Palestinian world beyond. It was the first time I had been involved in a daytime operation where there was no curfew.

No one paid any attention as our green vehicle trundled past them. Then the first rock hit the car, then another. I instinctively ducked. Boaz just grinned and said "assholes!" There were people walking around carrying textbooks and shopping bags. There were old people and a lot of young people about and in the middle of all this hustle and bustle I remember seeing one guy pick up a rock and throw it at us. I expected a full-scale riot to erupt at the presence of our vehicle but the people next to the man who threw the rock just looked embarrassed. The first rocks hitting the car scared me, but Boaz's calm demeanour reminded me that no one was throwing anything at the car that could cause it any damage. Strengthened by the knowledge I looked back out at the world with new eyes.

I pointed and stuck my tongue out at a man who was in the act of throwing a rock at us. He threw it anyway but a teenage boy next to him laughed. I carried on pulling funny faces for the rest of the drive. Some people threw stones, some people looked at the ground and some laughed.

We arrived at the designated house and our commandos walked out and bundled into the back of the car. I stopped making funny faces on the way back. My first encounter with Palestinians in daylight was over. I had found a strange kind of humanity over there though. Seeing someone smiling had surprised me far more than a few stones bouncing off the car.

25

FIRST ARREST, FIRST SUICIDE BOMBER

We moved into the city in convoy and stopped at our scheduled destination. The walk through the city was short this time and we arrived at the address quickly. In good order the team split into different squads, each tasked with covering a different part of the dwelling. Once the team was in position Black threw stones at the door to let those inside know we were there. Throwing stones at the door allowed him to keep a decent amount of distance between himself and the target house.

The door opened and a middle-aged woman stepped out. She wore a headscarf and was shouting in Arabic. We had an Arabic speaker with us and he shouted back at her. At his urging both the woman and a bunch of others left the dwelling behind and came out. Each was searched except the woman. The suicide bomber wasn't with them and the Arabic speaker had another word with the woman. Her voice rose and she gesticulated. I was kneeling at a corner to the address and could see her but hear very little.

The conversation continued. The whole family were involved now and everyone was talking over each other. There were five of them in total, two of them were clearly the parents and another three I assumed to be the kids. The youngest looked about nine. The Arabic speaker turned to the father and talked directly to him. When he finished the father got up and went back inside. When he came out he had the suicide bomber we had been looking for. He was a tall, clean-shaven man. He walked towards us with his eyes firmly planted on the ground.

The translator shouted at him and the man stopped. He lifted his shirt and turned around revealing himself to be devoid of an explosive vest. Once he had completed his twirl Tom and Liran went up to him, blindfolded him and cuffed him. He was led into the armoured car that had driven up to our position once we had made ourselves known. Then he was inside, then we were inside and the car was driving back to base with the bomber in our hands.

We all made our way back in two vehicles. The bomber was in the car with my squad while the rest of the team was in the second car. He was still blindfolded and cuffed as he sat there on the cold metal floor of the armoured vehicle. He said nothing as the car trundled along. I tried very much to feel hatred for him during that journey but I felt nothing. I just saw a man. I imagined the 20 or 30 people who wouldn't die because we had picked him up and felt like I had accomplished a holy act.

26

A MAN CALLED FUDDY BUDDY

Half my team had been sent off on a four-month course that would see them all qualify as squad leaders. I remained with the other eight members of my team. I knew that by not being on that course I was allowing my dream of an army career to slip through my fingers, but I didn't care. After a year of training I was finally going out on real missions and I wasn't willing to give that up.

At the base I slipped into the routine. We would go out on operations by night and do whatever we wanted during the day. The army was an entirely different animal once training was completed. No one wants to know you or talk to you while you're a trainee but as soon as you finish you become a 'real' soldier and are welcomed into the family that is the unit. Our area of the base was segregated from the rest and no one from the bigger army bothered us. The officers tended to spend each day planning that night's operation. This meant the rest of us got up when we pleased and there was no one in authority to order us around.

The food on the base was passable. When we were there on weekends the non-commissioned officer in charge of the kitchen would wander into our area of the base to recruit a volunteer to do the washing up. Because the Sabbath was a rest day no one did any washing up from Friday night at dusk until the same time on Saturday. Hundreds of soldiers had eaten at least three meals by this point. Their plates, cutlery and the enormous cauldrons and kitchen utensils used to cook the food were sitting on the floor of a filthy kitchen waiting to be scrubbed. So on Saturday we all knew a volunteer was going to have to go and each of us tried to get out of doing it.

Everyone seemed to know when the fat sergeant was on his way. By the time he arrived in our area everyone had disappeared into their shared rooms and shut the doors. There'd always be one unfortunate soul wandering around unaware of what was happening. He would be seized by the sergeant and no one would see him again for hours. It was so hard for that sergeant to find someone that when he did the soldier wasn't even excused from the kitchen to go out on that night's operation. I never had a problem roaming around Nablus but the prospect of being forced to clean pots and pans for hours on end filled me with dread.

It was at this time – around November 2003 – that we were tasked with arresting or killing a man named Fuddy Buddy. Every night this guy wandered around the kasbah of Nablus with an M16 rifle wearing a Kevlar helmet and a bulletproof vest. The man had even rustled up an IDF uniform. His plan was to infiltrate our patrols in the kasbah and start shooting. He was betting that his uniform wouldn't just allow him to confuse us but would ensure that after he started shooting no one would know who to shoot back at. The whole brigade was looking for him and one night it was our turn to try to pick him up.

I hadn't encountered a Palestinian warrior before. It had always been slightly shocked looking guys coming out of houses with their hands up. Often they managed to flee before we arrived. For me this was the chance I'd been waiting for. I wanted to find an enemy soldier to pit my skills against in a final test of all I'd learned. Since I finished training all I ever heard was soldiers talk about coming under fire and the battles they'd fought. I wondered when it would be my turn. Hearing about this character made me think of combat, glory and honour. I wanted to be the one to take his scalp. I didn't just want the man dead, I wanted to be the one to kill him.

The lights of the briefing room were darkened and all eyes were fixed on a projector screen. A map with the route for the coming operation was beamed onto it. It was the first operation we would be going on with a new commander of the unit. His name was Amit: he was a very different man from the gruff, authoritarian Coby he replaced.

The plan was simple enough. Intelligence said he was located at a certain address. We were to walk to the address and arrest him. To maintain surprise, the vehicles would drop us at the fringe of the city and we'd walk in. They told us we'd need a ladder to climb down to street level at a certain point along the way. We were given a collapsible ladder that a soldier could carry easily on his back. We practised wandering around with the ladder and assembling it in the dark. We also practised our general order of movement and when the time came we boarded the armoured cars for the short journey to the edge of Nablus.

The city of Nablus is built into a valley. We started at the top and spiralled our way down. The outskirts of the city looked like one enormous building site. Walking around the periphery I could see skeletons of small apartment buildings that had been abandoned during their construction. Some had plastic sheeting fluttering in the breeze, causing ripples of sound to carry over to us. We followed a dirt track down into the city. The occasional howl of a dog and the now familiar crackling sound of distant shooting floated over to us during our descent.

The winter cold hadn't yet set in, making movement easy, even pleasant. I saw no one as I walked with the butt of my rifle in my shoulder and finger on the trigger guard. I knew I was supposed to keep my attention on what was happening right in front of me but during that long walk down I couldn't stop thinking of other things. I thought of all the people in the world playing computer games pretending to do what I was doing for real. I thought of all my friends from England. I wondered how I could ever explain it to them. Some of them were doing graduate training schemes with banks; others had worked for a while and were now enjoying themselves travelling. I was wandering around Nablus looking for a terrorist.

As with my first time, I couldn't fail but note the difference between the quality of buildings at the edge of the city and in the centre. As we moved towards our objective everything became more dilapidated, wrecked, broken. The space between buildings shrank until it was gone altogether. Where the buildings were separated from one another it was often by tiny alleyways that one could barely walk through. Much of this part of the city was in disrepair. I guessed it was damage done during Operation Defensive Shield. Buildings were occasionally burned out; many were missing entire walls.

The lamp posts of the city shone neon white. These lamp posts were our enemies. They illuminated us and frustrated the effectiveness of night-vision goggles. If we were in a position under them we'd shoot the lights out. The soldier carrying the ladder on his back was called Avner, a kibbutznik from the south. He'd only been in the army four months longer than me but was so cocky you'd think he had been doing this for years. I was behind him and removed the collapsible ladder from his back. The two of us assembled it in a burnt-out building, two sides of which had been destroyed.

Moving through the building was only slightly tricky, with parts of the semi-collapsed building interfering with movement. We came out through to the other side to find a drop down to the street below. I marvelled at the local intelligence of the planners who insisted we take a ladder. The drop was about 10 feet. Directly opposite me, on the other side of the street was a big apartment building, built in the same haphazard way as the other buildings around me. It looked as if each successive floor had been thrown on as an afterthought to the original structure.

Avner had taken the ladder to our officer and the rest of us dropped to one knee in the half-light. The two of them lowered the ladder to the street below. Sweat trickled down into my eyes from the exertion of movement. I shivered a little as a gust of wind rushed through me. For some reason, I was looking to my left away from Avner and down the street below when the dirt next to me splashed up. Then I heard the shots. Bang bang bang bang bang bang bang. Seven shots fired in quick succession. The sound was abrupt; rudely slicing through the silence we had taken such care to safeguard.

I was disappointed. It was an instinctive feeling that overwhelmed me far more than the desire to find cover. Everyone else pressed themselves back against the building we had just moved through. I was there a moment longer, pondering the fact that I had just been shot at. Black was the only one in a position to fire back, the walls of the building kept us out of the shooter's line of sight and vice versa. His two shots penetrated the air a couple of seconds later.

Silence descended again. The unit just sat there waiting for orders. This was the first test of our new commander, Amit. What would he do? The static squelch of a radio transmission cut through the silence and a tall soldier emerged. The three members of his squad followed him. He winked at me as he walked past. He'd helped me with navigation training a few months earlier. His girlfriend had been killed in a suicide bombing not long before the mission. His men followed him. They looked alert and ready and tough. They knelt next to Amit while he gave them their orders and then they disappeared back in the direction we had come from.

I heard a shot. A crack through the night. A bullet ploughing through the silence. Then another one and after a moment another. I took pride in the sound of those shots. They were carefully fired, ponderous, thoughtful, well-aimed shots made by a well-practised hand. They were a world away from the seven shots that had made the dirt erupt next to me and hit no one.

Once our man had fired from his position we began to move.

Avner secured the ladder and we descended onto the street below. At the bottom of the ladder I took cover behind a car. I faced the direction the gunfire had come from and saw an arch passing over the street no more than 20 meters away from me. The arch was in fact someone's home that had been built over the street, connecting buildings on either side. The gunman must have fired at us from a window in that arch. I crouched behind the car trying to make out anyone through my night scope. There I sat. I waited. An order came down to go back up the ladder.

At the top I followed the others back to the skeletal building we had moved through earlier. I took a seat next to Uzi and we sat there wondering what was happening. From my seat I looked at the ledge where the bullets had kicked up dust. I recognised one of the guys crouching there, providing cover. He had been in the unit eight months longer than me. A wealth of experience could be amassed in eight months.

Silence was no longer with us. The murmur of people whispering to each other was like a small wave that lapped at me. I could make out vague voices though not the words.

Time passed. The veteran shifted; he had reached for something. He pulled the pin off a small canister and dropped it into the street below. A cloud of smoke drifted up, engulfing him completely. I heard someone I couldn't see shout, "WAKEF" (stop in Arabic). A red light illuminated the smoke. It came and it went, the glow from an ambulance. When it met the white mist it engulfed the crouching soldier first in a red glow and then left him as a black silhouette engulfed in white smoke. Arabic voices added to the sounds around me. A red laser beam from an emitter on the veteran's rifle pierced the smoke. Where the intermittent red glow was soft and wide, this beam was sharp, focussed. No one told me what was happening below. Then it was done. Our vehicles came and picked us up.

Once back at base Uzi told me that our sharpshooter, the one who had fired the shots I'd been so proud to hear, had hit a woman in the neck. He'd seen her peering through her blinds of her window – one of the windows in the archway the gunman had fired at us from. She'd been carrying a broom and peeking out after hearing the noise. Now she was dead. There was an inquiry into the killing. On a night operation we had come under fire and fired back. No soldier was hurt, no terrorist was hurt but a woman had been killed because she had been holding a broom and was in the wrong place at the wrong time. The marksman was found to have acted according to the demands of the situation. Had I been in his place I was sure I would have done the same thing. Meanwhile Fuddy Buddy had fired and fled. A couple of months later someone from the Sayeret shot him in the leg though he still managed to get away from them.

27

A WEEK IN NABLUS

Winter descended on Nablus though we weren't able to go out wearing cold weather clothing as the officers had decided it would restrict our movement. So when we went out at night we shivered. During the day it was still pretty warm, though, so we managed.

This mission was a brigade level one, which called for the whole of the Paratroopers to descend on Nablus and remain there for several days. Once there our specific task was to patrol the heart of the city by day and to lay ambushes by night. We took with us sandbags that had been filled with dirt at the base before leaving, we also brought all of the paraphernalia of soldiering that would be required such as a toasty machine and packets of yellow cheese and bread. Some genius had even rustled up a bottle of ketchup.

Our objective was an apartment block in the kasbah. We were to take over the whole building and use it as a base for a week or so. The families were moved from their apartments into the ground floor. Unpacking the armoured vehicles was done swiftly and we dived into the task of turning a regular apartment building into a fortified base. Various guard positions were constructed, camouflage netting was thrown up and sandbags were placed in front of windows. A large spool of barbed wire was laid out in front of the building.

Before long the necessary changes had been made leaving us free to attack the toasty machine with gusto. We had brought enough snacks with us for four days so within about an hour it was all gone. We went out on patrol that night listening to small arms fire, which was occasionally interrupted by larger calibre machine guns.

The next day we were up early and equipped with a bunch of addresses for house to house searches. The lists were provided by intelligence. It was still grey outside and so we put on thermal clothes under our uniforms. Technically we weren't allowed to but we put them on anyway. With body armour and combat vests on and weapons ready we entered the world outside to begin our sweep.

The streets were dead. All the men had been called to a central location and told to bring their ID cards. I marvelled at how different the place looked during the night versus during the day. I had come to know the city well but I had developed a nagging fear of getting separated from the rest of the guys. If that happened the chances were that I'd never be able to find my way out of the twists, turns and tunnels that constituted the old city of Nablus. Gunfire was so regular you tensed if it stopped rather than if it started.

We patrolled through the streets on such high alert that our officer blind fired a few rounds before every corner he turned. We covered various arcs as we moved. One would be covering up, another left or right and so on. Each of us was tensed for the fight that might or might not come as we moved through enemy turf. After minutes of this kind of movement and with the rising sun we were all awash in sweat.

The twisting and turning alleyways of the kasbah reminded me of the Old City of Jerusalem with their cramped spaces and homes seemingly built into each other. Sometimes we'd walk under homes built to bridge a street. Sometimes we would end up walking through whole alleyways that were turned into tunnels because people had built over any space they could find.

One place we needed to search was situated in such a tight street that Black went forward only with his own squad, sending each of his other squads to cover the entry to the alleyway. When he was in he called us over the radio to join him inside. Once in the home we swept through it. There wasn't much there, in fact it was barely big enough for us all to fit in it. There was a couple living there, both of whom were smiling at us, which struck me as bizarre. If soldiers were going through my house I would have been angry as hell I thought. It was only years later that I understood that they must have been afraid of us.

In one of the homes we had searched, someone asked Black if we could change out of our thermals. He said no, at which point we all started moaning and he realised his whole team was wearing them. So in a home we'd just searched, all 18 of us started undressing. Intelligence later informed us that at that moment the most wanted terrorist in the kasbah was in the dwelling next door listening to us through the paper-thin walls.

After moving through various homes on our list we arrived at one that was set around a courtyard. The open space was a welcome relief from the tight confines of the area we had been moving through. It was just a square of emptiness in an area of ancient, tight urban complexes. The only permanent structure was a kitchen; upon entering it I saw a toilet next to the gas oven and the kitchen counter. On another side there was a temporary structure made of wood with another toilet inside. On the western side was something that looked like a hut. Inside was a bed with a wood cupboard barely squeezed into the tiny space. Black suggested we crack open our rations and eat lunch.

There was a family of people there with us. An old woman wearing a headscarf, a younger woman similarly dressed and an older man wearing white robes that reminded me of the attire I had seen Pakistani men wear in London. It looked like a long dress with loose sleeves covering his arms. A plastic tube snaked its way from underneath the man's clothing up to a transparent colostomy bag he held in one hand. He held a cigarette in the other. The man continually paced back and forth carrying this bag while smoking cigarette after cigarette. The bag filled with urine. There were two kids – a little girl and a boy who must have been around eight or nine. The boy was light skinned in stark contrast to his family, his hair was black.

The others cracked open the food while sitting on a step that led into the kitchen/toilet. I opted to stand guard while they ate. The place had sapped my appetite. I looked around me, rifle strap around my neck and fingers lightly touching the handle of my weapon. The little girl played a game of her own invention that involved running from grown-up to grown-up oblivious to our presence. The man paced. His eyes would flicker up to me and the others and then back down again to the ground. The old woman sat on the dirt near the centre of the courtyard. She said nothing but constantly looked at me with pleading eyes, as if there was something I could or should be doing for them. A blue ball rolled over to my boot. The little kid had kicked it towards me. I knocked it back and he kicked it towards me again.

It's an unwritten rule that you're supposed to keep a stern demeanour when on an operation but a flicker of a smile moved across my lips as I played with this kid. The boy kicked the ball. The girl giggled and continued to bounce around between the adults. The sound of gunshots echoed around the homes of the kasbah while I played football with a Palestinian child. My eyes were drawn back to the old woman sitting there on the ground. Her look was as maddening as it was unyielding. She was demanding something from me with that look but I didn't know what it was. Her lips curled up at the sides almost like a smile. She held her arms out at her sides in an expression of sheer powerlessness while she rocked back and forth on the ground. I ignored her, but I couldn't forget her.

The guys finished eating and Black patted me on the back as I sent the little blue ball rolling along to the boy once again. "End your little peace process and let's go search the place," he said. We moved together to search the standalone bedroom. A double bed with a coarse brown blanket strewn across it occupied almost the entire room. The big wooden cupboard faced it. We rummaged through the drawers. I found several expired green Jordanian passports and some bed linen. I looked at Black to signal I was done with my search. He nodded his head and we both left. It was strange being so equal with him after a year of having him look down at me. Increasingly I felt like we were two flies stuck in the same web together.

Back in the courtyard the rest of the guys were already standing up ready to move on. I took a last look at the place. I remember thinking that if those people left and took nothing at all with them they would be no poorer: that man with his grimace and his colostomy bag, the kids smiling over nothing, the boy kicking the ball to me. It was the old woman using the ground for a chair and with a practised face of helplessness who imprinted herself on my consciousness. There was no one to help them, not us, not their own leaders, not the UN, not the volunteers from Europe or America, no one to respond to her silent pleas for help.

28

ARE THEY THROWING STONES?

We were sent home after that week of operations. I had the beach, the bars, takeout pizza and anything else I wanted. Except that my rifle was locked away in my apartment and my friends weren't around to back me up anymore. The terrorists I was going out every night to catch were trying to get past me into the very place I had now been sent to "relax". It was almost worse to be allowed to go home than it was to be in the field.

A day or two away from the streets of Nablus was enough time to remind me a world existed without the constant popping of gunfire in the background. Just long enough to remember that some people worked in offices and existed in a world of bars and parties and restaurants. But it wasn't enough time to get used to it. I mostly just slept.

I returned to the army to hear that we had a new sergeant and a new mission. The sergeant's name was Motti – a blond-haired, blue-eyed boy from a religious moshav in the centre of Israel. The mission was to close down Nablus. The whole Paratrooper brigade, along with some tanks, was being sent in to enforce a daytime curfew.

There had been a slow increase in enemy activity over the previous weeks and, evidently, someone high up felt it was necessary to move into the city and lock it down. There were no house-to-house searches or any other missions timetabled. The operation was simply to be there. We were split into squads and each squad was assigned a vehicle. Each vehicle was to sit on a junction and close it to traffic. No civilians were allowed onto the streets. Most important of all, it was all going to take place during the day.

I imagined that terrorists were more likely to come out of the woodwork and shoot at us while we were holding individual junctions. It meant we'd be static and they'd know how to get us. The realization released a free flow of adrenaline that had me buzzing.

After the briefing we all headed back to our corner of the base to prepare our equipment. It had become my ritual. I'd check that my grenades were in place in the pouches above my magazines. I would check that the Velcro straps for my combat vest were clean and free of any blades of grass trapped in the black fabric. I made sure my medical kit was in place next to my grenades high up in my vest. I checked the batteries for my night scope and that I had spares. It was a daylight operation but I always brought the scope with me just in case. While going through my equipment I would always play out scenarios in my mind as to what might happen and how I would react to any challenges. My biggest fear was always that I would fail to react quickly enough to help my friends if someone really did start shooting at us.

Once the ritual was complete I stepped outside for some air and bumped right into Motti. My jaw dropped to see him unloading crate after crate of non-lethal ammunition from a truck. There were stun grenades, tear gas grenades, smoke grenades, special non-lethal ammunition for underslung grenade launchers and much, much more. "Marc, have you ever used one of these before?" he asked, handing me a six-inch-long black cylinder. It looked just like a silencer.

He tossed it to me before I could answer and I caught it with one hand. It was heavier than it looked. Motti told me to empty one of my magazines and load it with blanks. "It fires these," he said while reaching into one of the ammunition boxes and pulling out a plastic packet of what looked like four rubber cylinders. I pulled one out of the box and took a closer look. There were four sticks of pellets in the packet. Each stick consisted of four smaller pellets; each pellet was a centimetre in length.

"You open the packet and take one of the tubes, then you load the stick of four into the tube you have attached to the end of your rifle and pull the trigger," Motti stated matter-of-factly. The pellets were rubber bullets. I had always thought that rubber bullets worked the same way as actual bullets but were simply made of rubber, particularly since news services often referred to them as "rubber coated steel bullets". In fact they are small rubber cylinders and they are fired from a tube at the end of a rifle.

Other soldiers gathered around, we were all looking at this candy store of equipment. None of the guys in my team had ever used this stuff before. Now they were handing them out by the dozen. There were crates of munitions being divided up between the vehicles that each six-man squad would be in the next day. It hammered home the message that there was going to be trouble.

That night I lay in my bunk wondering what awaited me in Nablus the next day. For years I had wanted to be in a battle. I wanted my equivalent of the storming of the temple mount by the Paratroopers of 1967. I thought of all of the old warriors from World War II and Vietnam I had seen on television. They all said things like "if you weren't scared there was something wrong with you" or "I had no idea what I was getting into" or "the only heroes are the dead ones". Well, I wasn't scared, I wanted to fight. I wanted to know what it was they were talking about. I had spent a year being prepared for war and had yet to experience one. Having seen all the ordnance loaded into the vehicles I imagined that the next day I might experience something close.

We rose before dawn the next day to arrive at our assigned junctions before the city awoke. I had emptied two magazines and filled them both up with blanks ready to fire rubber bullets with. Whatever was waiting for me at the end of the journey I was determined to fulfil our mission. I sat crouched in the armoured car as the driver gunned the engine into life and raced us into Nablus before sunrise. We arrived minutes later at our assigned junction.

We sat at our empty junction in Nablus at 4 a.m. in the dark. Everyone in the city was still asleep. Excitement turned to boredom, which turned to frustration. A blue armoured jeep from the border guard parked alongside us. They had a loudspeaker attached to their vehicle broadcasting a message in Arabic telling the residents of the city to stay indoors and to respect the curfew. I imagined that what they were doing was waking everyone up and telling them we were there. I didn't mind, I had come ready for a riot. I eyed the crates of munitions wondering when I would have the opportunity to use them, wondering when I would see some action.

The hours passed. The jeep drove around blaring out the same words over and over again. "There's a curfew, stay home, don't come outside." It was cramped in the armoured car. You couldn't pace around, obviously; you couldn't stand up either; you couldn't do anything except sit. With nothing to do and no end in sight the vehicle became smaller and smaller with the passage of time. I just sat there eyeing up all the equipment. The heat grew heavier as the sun came out. Trouble would at least mean the chance to get out of the vehicle.

I thought back to the briefing, to the words of the commander, to his talk of snipers and rioters. All that lay outside were empty streets, while crates of rubber bullets, gas grenades, stun grenades and other weapons lay inside. Time ticked by. Where was everyone? Let there be a riot or let them send us back to base! Four o'clock in the morning became five, which became six and then seven and then eight. All the time we sat in the vehicle looking at each other.

Many of the soldiers in the unit had participated in

Operation Defensive Shield and had come as close to war as anyone. Compared to them we were untested in combat. I felt the older veterans looking at us and I wanted the whole unit to know my team and I were dependable under fire. I wanted the experience of being in a riot, I wanted to prove to myself that I could handle it, that I could be cool under the fire of an attacking mob. But there was no attacking mob. The streets were deserted.

We moaned to each other, we talked about nothing and everything and shifted positions trying to get comfortable while wearing our bulletproof vests with our equipment vests over them. Slowly, slowly, outside the armoured car civilians began their daily routines. We could see people moving around though they were giving our vehicle a wide berth. Motti ordered me outside. This was it! This was my moment. I kicked open the rear door of the vehicle while Motti exited from the passenger seat at the front.

A large number of people had gathered about 50m away from us. They were breaching the curfew. Now what do I do? Should I shoot rubber bullets at them? This was the time to start shooting. Wasn't it? Wasn't our brigade level operation happening specifically to stop people from leaving their houses? Well here they were and here we were, let's stop them!

Everyone was ignoring the curfew completely. But there was no hostility. The people kept their distance to about 50 meters but they were breaking the curfew we were supposed to be imposing! Motti stood there looking at them. I scanned the windows of the apartment buildings around us for snipers. He carried on watching. Finally I said; "I think I should shoot rubber bullets at them." He looked at me. "Motti they're breaking the curfew!" I said. I nearly shouted it at him. I couldn't stop thinking about our mission. We were failing to achieve our objective! We were failing to keep the streets clear of people! The rest of the unit was watching us!

Motti sighed a little and turned to me, "Fire one rubber

bullet towards the crowd." My time had come! I dropped to one knee, opened a packet of rubber bullets placed them in the tube and took aim. But who to aim at? There were people wandering around quite slowly, happily ignoring us and me. I picked a man walking while holding a box and fired. There was a bang but no visible effect. The man carried on walking. I checked my weapon in confusion.

The weapon had fired the rubber bullets, but they simply failed to make it the distance. The effect on the people moving was minimal: they sped up a little but I could see them slowing down again the moment they felt they were out of range. We were still failing in our mission. Uzi rolled down the front window, "I think I should fire gas at them from my grenade launcher," he said. Motti shook his head. "Seriously Motti," he added, "they're not going home, they're breaking curfew!" Motti still didn't let him shoot.

No one around us was committing any violence. I didn't feel threatened standing there in the open. Which was weird because it was enemy territory. It was Nablus, city of the suicide bombers, and it was daylight. I had hoped the armed men of the Al Aqsa Martyrs Brigades would start shooting, allowing us a real taste of combat. But they weren't playing ball.

The junction we were located at remained clear of people, however, 50m away another one was becoming busier all of the time. Our presence didn't seem to change anything. "Fire the rubber bullets at them again," Motti said. Again I fired; again I hit nothing. No one paid any attention or even looked in my direction. How could these people not understand? News of the curfew was broadcast on the radio, they all knew and yet here they all were with more gathering all the time. Again I knelt; again I fired. I was rewarded by seeing a small dispersal. It lasted moments. We were still failing. Frustration coursed through me as if it were a chemical in my blood.

"I think I need to fire again," I said. It was beyond my comprehension that people would still be running around even though I was firing rubber bullets at them. How were they still going on as if nothing was happening? Instead of fewer people more were gathering. I wasn't afraid I was confused. What were they all doing? I kept looking at Motti for guidance, presently he threw a stun grenade at the people moving through the junction before us. The bright orange plastic cylinder flew through the air towards the junction and exploded on the ground with a flash of light and loud BANG but nothing else. It was as painfully ineffective as the rubber bullets had been.

"Okay get back in the car," said Motti. I jumped back in and as soon as the doors were closed our driver stepped on the gas and took us right into the offending junction. "Okay get out and get a stun grenade ready."

Motti jumped out from the front and I jumped out the rear, stun grenade in hand. "Throw it," he said. I looked left and right at this new reality. Now people were very near. I threw the grenade into a clump of people about 20 meters away and watched them run from it just before it blew up. Then they carried on as before. No one was going home. It was infuriating. We were right there, we were armed to the teeth, we were shooting rubber bullets at them and we were throwing stun grenades at them and they weren't going home! There was no fighting, there was no stone throwing just people going about their business as if we didn't exist.

Then I heard Uzi …"I think I should fire gas at them," he offered.

"No, it's too close," Motti said.

So we just stood there, my mouth agape at the fact that no one even seemed to notice us. I felt out of place with my rifle and my rubber bullets, my stun grenades and helmet, while all these people were wandering in their civilian clothes with shopping bags, briefcases and other detritus of civilian life. We shouted and gesticulated and the armoured car drove around blaring out the message to go home. Nobody did. I hadn't once imagined a situation where we would be confronted by indifference. Was I supposed to start shooting with live rounds to disperse everyone?

Now people were coming through small alleyways and side roads all around us. It seemed counter-intuitive to do anything other than run as far away from us as possible but they all just ignored us. "Uzi, you can fire a gas grenade at the junction we just left," Motti said. Finally with an excuse to get out of the armoured car, Uzi jumped down, loaded the gas grenade into his underslung launcher and fired. The thick, green gas had an immediate effect. People ran leaving that junction clear once again.

Uzi then pointed out a hill filled with people on the move. Those who had abandoned one junction had simply moved over to another. He wanted to fire a gas grenade at the crowd from where we were. Motti gave him permission to fire. He loaded the shell into his underslung M203 launcher, aimed and fired. The resulting gas wafted up on the face of the hill that the people had been walking along. I could see people walking up to the gas cloud, running through it and then walking once again. The wind would disperse the gas in moments; we hadn't achieved a thing. Uzi fired again, then I heard him laughing, "Shit man, I just hit one of them on the head!" I cracked a smile too. The power was intoxicating. The humour was like Charlie Chaplin or Tom and Jerry violence. It was happening but in a way that was utterly removed from us even though we were causing it.

It turns out that we were located next to a school and there were several parents arriving with young children with their little backpacks on. We ordered them home. They did leave us but it seemed that for every one who left more people arrived. The junction was by now entirely abuzz with people, activity and movement to a level that had overwhelmed us. Throughout the morning there hadn't been the slightest sign of hostile activity. I had long since stopped telling Motti that I should be firing something at them, despite the fact that we had demonstrably failed in our mission. This went on until it became clear that, short of using live rounds, we weren't going to have any effect on the movement of civilians in the city.

I remember a well-dressed man walking up to me and presenting me with a letter in Arabic that he said came from the UN and was a permit for him to leave the city. I gave him his letter back and shrugged. What made me remember him was by how carefully he folded it back up and placed it into the envelope from which he had taken it. For me it was a piece of paper; for him it was a treasured document.

I stood there, grim faced, waving people away unsure how I was supposed to accomplish my mission. The sneaking suspicion grew with each passing civilian that the objective was an un-achievable one. The thrill of firing new weapons and grenades turned into frustration at their lack of effect. I felt ridiculous for having so much as considered the possibility of entering into battle that day. Eventually the number of people thinned out and we all sat in the back of the armoured car and opened a ration pack for lunch.

We finished eating and just sat there. The operation continued but our neighbourhood had thinned out. I said to myself "mission accomplished" but I didn't care anymore. What had the mission even been? To keep everyone in their house? I had expected a riot and shooting, maybe even a full-fledged battle for Nablus. Instead there had been regular people dropping kids off at school. No snipers, no Molotov cocktails, no action, no combat, no glory.

The heat inside the armoured car grew. The vehicle by now was full of empty packaging and leftover food. I hadn't been able to remove any of my equipment for hours. The first lesson I learned after training was that my own frustrations and thoughts were irrelevant. Someone much higher up than me was making plans and decisions based on the various units under his command. All we could do was sit in that vehicle and wait until we were ordered to do something. We talked until we ran out of things to say. Then we sat in silence.

I thought of my friends in the UK. The last I heard, three of them were backpacking their way around Australia, another one was halfway through medical school, another was about to finish his law conversion. My friend Alan was fulfilling his second term as president of the Union of Jewish Students in the UK. My journey had brought me to the stinking inside of an armoured car and a meal of beans and tuna eaten out of tins. I was sitting in a Palestinian city, wearing Israeli boots and carrying an American gun. I was being paid a couple of hundred pounds a month. My own personal graduate programme.

This stinking armoured car and the stinking people in it and the Palestinians outside, who were ignoring us today and blowing us up tomorrow. This was the dream I had come to Israel for. There was no battle and there was no glory left to be had. I had earned a red beret, the paratrooper's silver wings and the paratrooper's red boots. Now I had the Paratrooper's job; to sit in Nablus in an armoured car and wait without knowing what it was I was even waiting for. To be honest it still seemed like a better deal than spending my life sitting in a bank wondering what would have happened if I'd dared to follow my dreams.

The radio screeched orders to move to another junction. An armoured car from the newest team to finish training had come 'under fire' from stone throwers and we were to replace them and restore calm. Stone throwers weren't terrorists but they weren't civilians either. They threw stones and we had our non-lethal ammo to fire back at them. The closer we drove towards our newly allocated position the more the condition of the road deteriorated. At first it was only small stones but soon it became huge lumps of concrete covering the road's surface.

We found the rookies; their situation was hectic. The street was narrow with gangs of kids in both directions throwing stones, bottles and anything else they could move. Then they disappeared up to the roofs and started throwing things down on us from there. I felt the familiar waves of adrenaline flow through me. They weren't real terrorists, but certainly violent enough to have some fun with … enough that I could prove to my friends what a great soldier I was.

I broke open one of three cartons. Packed inside were powerful cylinders of explosive and rubber pellets. I unscrewed the black tube, which had remained attached to my weapon since early that morning. I replaced my half-empty magazine with a fresh one of blanks and pulled back the cocking handle once more. Now I was ready. When I next pulled the trigger the explosive inside the fat grey cylinder on the end of my weapon would be ignited by the gas produced by the blank and a hundred or so rubber pellets would be pushed out as though I were firing a non-lethal shotgun.

The driver pulled our vehicle up next to that of the rookies so that Motti could speak to their officer. They had to shout at one another over the racket of stones and rocks pelting our vehicles. The rookies sped off leaving us to it. The road we were on was on the side of a hill, so there were houses to the left of the vehicle and a sharp dip down to the right. The homes on the road had no gaps between them, allowing stone throwers to run the length of the street without ever having to leave the rooftops. One end of the street was blocked by burning tyres. After the hours of nothing in the morning here was something that looked more like action. There was danger; there was excitement. There was the chance to do something that looked a little bit like soldiering.

I kicked open the back door of the armoured car and fired the rubber bullet shotgun upwards towards the roof. I was rewarded with instant silence. The stone throwers ran back from the edge of the roof and out of sight. It gave me time to reload.

Then the first brick came from far back on the roof. Thrown blind it hit the side of the road just near me. Then another and another and another until it was raining stones once again. I ducked back inside the vehicle. The pelting rocks made a sound on the reinforced steel of the vehicle similar to rain on glass.

We sat there for a moment planning what our next move should be. Then we all jumped out of the vehicle and fired at the same time. The rocks and rubble stopped coming for a moment as the stone throwers once again ran off out of sight. "You sons of bitches!" I screamed. Everyone looked at me. I shrugged. This was my moment and I was determined to exude coolness and action-hero nonchalance. A moment or two passed and again bricks and stones fell at us from the air. I already had another canister on the end of my rifle and scoured the rooftops for sight of the people throwing stuff at us. I didn't have a chance to fire; "Oh shit everyone back in the vehicle. Now!" Motti said. "Marc get in!" he shouted as I lingered trying to get a shot off.

The stone throwers also stopped. A lull descended. I turned to Motti but he just pointed out the window. A white armoured jeep appeared. At first I thought it was the UN, but as it came closer I could make out the letters "TV" taped onto the bonnet with black tape.

The jeep drove into the scene, slowly cruising along the debris littered street, across and over our battlefield. They came uninvited into our battlefield. The car drove all the way up to the burning tyres at the end of the street, then turned around and drove back down to the other end, before repeating the exercise. Again and again the wheels turned and the vehicle rolled around, in no hurry at all. Who did these TV people think they were to be driving our turf? I wondered.

This patch belonged to me and my squad and the stone throwers above. Whatever was happening, whatever we were fighting over was between us. The arrival of these TV people was an intrusive act. But there was no longer anything for them to film. The stones had stopped falling and we soldiers had shut ourselves into our vehicle. No matter how long the car stayed, no matter how long this white beast prowled no one broke the ceasefire. Slowly, ever so slowly, the driver made his final turn and drove off. No sooner had he done so than we heard the sound of rocks hitting the vehicle once again. Game on.

I knew the stone throwers had felt the same sense of imposition I had. It was as if two brothers had immediately quit fighting upon hearing the approach of a parent. As soon as the footsteps diminished we started fighting again in the knowledge that we were free from condemnation. When I looked down the small incline we had driven up to get to the street I saw a flaming barricade of tyres. Now we couldn't drive in either direction and for the first time I felt a pang of fear. Our stocks of non-lethal ammo were running low. Five rapid-fire gunshots coming from very nearby made it seem as if someone hit the reset button, game over. Everyone disappeared and silence once again reined. It was Uzi, who had fired at a nearby wall. It was as if the live gunfire was the timeout signal.

Then there was a huge thud. It hadn't been an explosion – something heavy had hit us. The driver reversed. Not easy to do with all the debris on the ground. The rugged vehicle managed it though and after a moment a washing machine fell from the roof of the vehicle. We all looked at each other with stupid half grins on our faces. How on earth had they managed to throw a washing machine at us? While we were scratching our heads a fat, middle-aged man walked towards our vehicle gesticulating wildly. Clearly he had something to say so I pushed the door open and he shouted over to us. Uzi translated as best he could and said that he was talking about his house. He was shouting up at the roof of a building rather than at us.

The driver reversed until we were close enough to hear what he was saying. Uzi listened and translated. I was getting impatient.

"What's he saying?" I begged of him.

"The washing machine, it's his," he said.

It turned out that the stone throwers had taken over his house and had spent the day throwing his possessions at us from his roof. All he could do was stand a safe distance away and watch as these kids threw the contents of his home at us. When he saw the washing machine thrown from the roof he couldn't wait any longer and had begun screaming up at the stone throwers to leave.

After mutual recriminations the man stormed into his house only to run out again coughing and with his eyes streaming tears. It was from gas Uzi had fired in an attempt to hit the stone throwers. He recovered after a couple of minutes and shouted up again to the people on the roof. The entire time this was going on we were being ignored. We could hear curses rain down from the roof in Arabic as thickly as the stones, glass, metal pipes and kitchen utensils had before. Then there was silence and the man walked away. We braced ourselves for a resumption of hostilities when, without warning, a door down the street opened and seven youths walked out staring at the ground. They varied in age from early adolescence to late teens. A couple wore scarves over their faces, others hoods from their sweaters. We watched them walk away in silence not believing it was possible for it all to end so innocuously. One of them threw a glance at me. We made eye contact then he jerked his eyes back to the ground. They walked down the hill, past the smouldering tyres to another junction. From our vantage point on the hill, we watched them move into another house and a previously quiet junction erupted. Ours remained silent.

The rubble-strewn road served as the only evidence that anything had happened. Motti and I stepped onto the road and watched civilians scuttle around again now that the road was clear. I looked away from the houses and noticed that the makeshift barricade had burned itself out as though a metaphor of the fury that had now disappeared.

Uzi called to me and I left the street for the safety of the car. I sat there with my friends talking about what had happened and joking about our near misses as well as marvelling at how they had managed to get a washing machine up to the roof. Eventually it began to get dark and it became time to leave the city. On the way back I leaned over to Uzi, "When you hit the guy on the head with the gas grenade why did you laugh?" He looked me right in the eye, "Because it was funny," he said.

The fact that I smiled along with him stayed with me. Even the stone throwers hadn't knocked it from me. As a point of fact the stuff with the stone throwers had been a lot of fun. I had stood there screaming obscenities at them before each time I fired. I wondered why. I kept thinking of a picture I had seen of a Nazi pointing his rifle at a woman at point blank range while she was holding a small child in her arms. The Nazi was smiling as he was doing it. Uzi had laughed and I had smiled when someone was hit on the head, because it was funny. But why? Why was it so fucking funny?

I felt as though my inner sadist had been released that day. We were divorced from the consequences of our actions. Watching someone get hit on the head by his grenade was the same for Uzi as watching someone get hit on the head in a cartoon. You smile because you don't know how else to react. As a soldier the last thing you want to do is show weakness so you show the opposite, as if to say this stuff affects me so little I can even smile and laugh about it. I thought back to that picture a great deal. Beforehand it had been all too easy to dismiss people as psychopaths but they weren't. It was what happened to anyone when they were released from all inhibitions, when everyone around them tells them something is okay – good even. You start to push the boundaries, find out just how much it is you're allowed to do.

I kept that picture of the Nazi in my head often; it was my reminder of just how fucked up people can be. In truth all we had done was fire non-lethal ordnance that day but the experience served as a reminder for the rest of my service that the only person who could hold a sense of proportion over my actions was me. Being handed rubber bullets and told to keep a junction clear of people was akin to being handed chopsticks and told to clean a house. It couldn't be done.

29

THE VILLAGE NEAR QALQILYA

After a few weeks we were rotated out of Nablus and back to our home base but the operations continued each night. The bus would arrive and transport us to the nearest base to our target. From there it would be an armoured car ride to the house where – according to intelligence – the terrorist we were picking up was hiding out. We weren't always active in Nablus, the operations took place in various parts of the West Bank. The most memorable mission from that time was in a small village next to Qalqilya. The city is located very close to the Israeli city of Netanya and sits at the narrowest point of Israel's waist a mere 16km from the sea. The village nearby was housing a local terrorist leader and we were being sent to pick him up.

It was a tense moment in the al Aqsa Intifada. A suicide bomber had just detonated himself in a café in Haifa and killed 21 people, including a retired admiral together with his wife, their son and their two young grandsons. The news at this time was full of shootings and bombings to the point at which people wanted to simply stop watching, but they couldn't. People in the unit were constantly scanning through the newspapers for lists of the dead and wounded to find out if they knew any of them. It was one of the good things about being a lone soldier. I never had to worry that any of my family would get killed.

This time the plan called for a trek through the countryside surrounding the village. The sound of the armoured cars would alert anyone and everyone for miles around that we were coming. Once in the village we would split into our squads, surround the house and out the terrorist would come with his hands up. That was the plan.

So that night I was trekking through the countryside, rifle in hand with night scope attached as per usual. The armoured cars had dropped us off relatively far away and we were moving in one long column towards our target. The closer we came to the village the slower and more careful became our movement. As we arrived at the first buildings on the outskirts of the village a dog I couldn't see started barking – first one lone, invisible dog and then a cacophony of animal roars. The guards had done their job; we were exposed. As one we sped up our movement towards the village. As we did so the barks of the dogs turned into the much more human sounds of wolf whistles at which point we were sprinting – speed became more important than caution.

I ran forward with Uzi behind me and the squad leader in front. He led us through the village and around the back of the houses. We rushed with the barking and the catcalling all around. Dawn hadn't yet broken as we jumped over walls and rushed around houses until we made it to our assigned position. Upon arrival, I trained my rifle on the building nearby, Uzi covered the direction we had just come from and the leader of our little squad, a soldier named Giora, remained next to me.

We couldn't see much in the dark, save for the target building before us. We were located at the rear and not even a light emanated from the flat-roofed house where the terrorist was supposed to be. Giora informed the commanders that we were in position and then we sat and waited. I thought of the SWAT guys you see in the movies. Not the hero, but the hundreds of guys with rifles who turn up and just sit on the periphery. They tend to get filmed for just a moment when they show up and then ignored. That was me. Just sitting on the outside pointing my rifle at a big house in front of us that was mainly obscured by the undergrowth around me.

The barking of the dogs died down, as did the wolf whistles.

There was no need for them anymore, Amit's team announced their presence in Arabic through a loudspeaker. I had no idea what was happening around the front of the building. Dawn broke, the sun came up and I switched from my night scope to my day scope. Uzi started nodding off behind me, I elbowed him every once in a while. He did the same to me.

Then there was radio traffic. A Kalashnikov assault rifle had been thrown off the roof. We didn't see it. There was more radio traffic. The hours continued to move by. The sun was up, it was turning into a hot day, the sun hadn't quite realised summer was over. Still we remained there. The radio allowed bits of information in between bursts of static. There was some kind of standoff going on. The terrorist wasn't coming out and we weren't going in. Eventually, with the sun climbing ever higher, the order to come around to the front of the house screeched through on the radio. We looked at one another and made our way around to the front of the building. There we saw the terrorist, he was on his knees, hands bound behind his back and blindfolded. Awesome. Can we go home now? I thought but didn't say.

Arresting this terrorist must have been a bigger event than I thought. The commander of the battalion rode into town to see him in person. The other reconnaissance units had hit the village as well, each hitting different locations since intelligence wasn't sure on exactly which building the guy was in. As it turned out, he was in ours. I looked him up and down. It was hard to perceive him as much of a threat; he looked like a kid. The difference was particularly pronounced with a couple of our guys standing next to him guarding him. He sat there head down, forlorn. He looked like he was about 16 years old, a small 16. I couldn't imagine him being particularly dangerous. I had learned enough to know that the way you look is utterly irrelevant.

The battalion commander was standing there looking at him. His name was "Schmulik". He looked him up and down and said to the guys guarding him, "Guard him well, he's a dangerous one." He then looked at Amit and said, "Search the whole village." And there it was, my hopes of getting back to base dashed. The fact that a Kalashnikov had been found at the scene was enough for a search of the whole area in the hope of finding more weapons.

The village was divided up into sections and each squad was given a section to search. Black came along with us as we traipsed through the village. We moved from door to door looking for guns. We'd knock on the door, the person would open, and in we'd walk and conduct our search. One door was opened by a young mother with her baby. We marched in and started looking through the cupboards and various potential hiding places. After clearing the downstairs, we went upstairs and started rummaging around there too. Giora saw a basket filled with washing and emptied it to find that within the basket was indeed just washing. One of the guys in another room knocked something over and the woman downstairs started screaming. It wasn't like a movie scream. It came in three short bursts and was a deeper sound than a scream – something between a scream and a shudder. I had never heard a sound like it before.

"Don't tear the place down, just look for guns!" came Black's voice from downstairs. Giora and I looked at one another, wondering what to do next. We shrugged and walked downstairs announcing that there were no guns to be found. It was frustrating; clearly someone hiding weapons wasn't simply going to leave them in a laundry basket, but by the same token we were hardly going to start tearing into the walls and looking for cavities in the home. It made me wonder why we were bothering.

There was a small shack just outside the woman's house and we walked in. It was filled with olives; the smell was the same as gas but about a hundred times stronger. I felt my stomach contract in revulsion. "Giora get in there and search the olives," Black barked. I said nothing. If there were guns in there then under the olives made sense. In Giora walked, gagging at the smell. It was when he started moving as if to vomit that I backed out of the room and Black showed some mercy, telling him it was enough.

That was one house. There was a whole village left to search, or at least our whole section of village. The bigger homes were on the fringe of the village, the closer you were to the centre the smaller and more dilapidated they became. We were working out from the centre, so the first houses were small and took less time to get through. In one of them a picture of a rifle had been drawn in black crayon on the wall. The family were standing together in a bunch. A man, a woman, three children. The arms of their parents on them. Black turned to them, "What's this?" he said, pointing at the wall. I rolled my eyes and then focussed them on their young son – he was about eight or nine. The woman smiled weakly at Black and shrugged in sort of a hopeless fashion under his stare.

"Black, it's clear," I said. The whole house amounted to about one room with no décor at all save for the fact their kid had drawn a picture of a gun in crayon. I wanted to leave that room. I wanted to leave the village. The job was done. Bad guy caught. The battalion commander said we had to search the village. I didn't know why or what we were looking for but I knew that we weren't equipped to test for openings between walls or secret compartments. I knew that we weren't trained in how to do it and there was no intelligence offered to us that there were weapons there.

I could imagine a scene. It was in the post operation debriefing where all of the higher ups patted themselves on the backs for a job well done. I could imagine Schmulik telling his bosses how he had ordered us into the village and caught the bad guy. I could imagine the moment when the Brigadier said something like; "So you found a rifle there, did you look for any more?" I imagined we were searching the village so that Schmulik could answer that question if it was asked. Maybe I was being too harsh on the guy.

When the search was called off we were transported back to base by a hulk of a vehicle nicknamed a "safari". This was essentially a lorry whose trailer was a heavily armoured space for soldiers to sit in while it made its way at a top speed of about 30 miles per hour. It was my first experience of such a vehicle and I immediately missed the dinky 'Knight' armoured cars that had been so reliable up to that point. But then no one asked me which vehicle I wanted to head back to base in.

I climbed on board with a bunch of other guys from the unit and the vehicle began its slow, lumbering journey back to base. The route seemed to involve moving solely along dirt tracks. Every moment, I expected the vehicle to tip over on one side or another as it plodded forward with its huge wheels on tiny paths. The metal heaved and groaned in pain at the fact that it was being forced along these inadequate surfaces. Inside we groaned right there along with it as we were thrown about like a box of human lego bricks being shaken by a toddler.

There is an opening at the back of these safaris, but no door. To prevent undesirables from throwing things directly into the back of the vehicle the opening has a huge slab of metal about 45cm wide that goes all of the way up to the roof. So when trying to get in one is immediately presented with this slab of metal and needs to manoeuvre around it. I was told to remain standing between the slab and the opening itself to make sure that no one was attempting to attack us from behind. So there I stood, almost falling out of the Safari as it lurched over the dirt tracks around and behind Palestinian villages and towns.

I stood there at the back of the vehicle watching as we drove past isolated homes. Sometimes a knot of three or four houses appeared together at the side of the pathway. In the main I didn't see any people, just the occasional goat. There was nothing going on, the fatigue had long since set in and keeping my eyes open wasn't easy. Then we arrived at a big white building with a fence separating it from the road. A load of kids ran up to the fence and I figured the building for a school. They looked like they ranged in age from five to ten. The kids ran away from the fence and a moment later a shower of rocks and broken bottles rained down upon us. I ducked back inside the protected vehicle, listening to the glass break on the armour plate. Someone I didn't know simply said "school?" I nodded and everyone else laughed. I had learned a new lesson the exact same way they had learned it. I cautiously peeked out of the back while the safari lazily, seemingly nonchalantly, continued on, impervious to the rocks and glass making their presence felt only by the noise of their impact.

30

BIRTHRIGHT

Birthright is the name of a programme that provides Jews who have never been to Israel with a free tour of the country. The trip lasts ten days and a group of Israeli soldiers join them. The idea is for the American Jews to meet some Israelis and spend some quality time with them, gaining them a fuller picture of Israeli society. I'd heard of Birthright but had no idea soldiers were sent to spend time with the groups. So it was with some surprise that I found myself plucked away from operations in Nablus and sent on an all-expenses paid tour of Israel. I didn't complain.

We were introduced to the group and then the four of us who had been sent from the army sat in a row. Then we asked each other questions. One of the guys from the Sayeret asked the group what they thought of us Israeli soldiers. I didn't need them to answer, I knew they thought we were the heroes. To them my 5'6" looked ten feet tall. One of the Americans in the group unashamedly said it too; "You're heroes," everyone giggled and we smiled. But I didn't feel much like a hero. It was strange to be on the other side of this. When I lived in the UK I had often looked at Israeli soldiers and thought of them as heroes: the Jews who carried weapons and held their heads up high.

We wandered around the country seeing the sites. We went to Masada and I heard again about the Jews who killed themselves en masse rather than be taken prisoner by the Romans and become slaves. We went rafting in the upper Galilee and we got drunk every night. These American college kids revelled in the opportunity to gorge themselves legally on alcohol. I remember one night looking at the bar and there was a kid lying on it while another opened the beer tap directly into his mouth until he choked.

Feelings of guilt that I was enjoying luxury hotels and nature walks while my tzevet were rolling through Nablus, or some other town – rifles in hand – plagued me. I missed the clarity of operations. Shoot or don't shoot. Arrest or don't arrest. During ops nothing mattered except the moment. Thanks to the army I rarely needed to think about such things as love and sex but on this Birthright group it was all about things like love and sex and having fun. But I wasn't sure I knew how to have fun in that way anymore.

The second most memorable part of the tour was watching them all get excited about seeing a donkey with an erection. They took photos of it and laughed and pointed. I watched them as if through a microscope and wondered what it was that separated me from them. My university days were only a couple of years before. Getting drunk and laughing about meaningless nonsense was something that should have come naturally. Once it had. But for that whole trip, though I had got drunk right alongside them, where they had become happy, I had become morose. While they had thought of fucking and stupid pranks, I had thought only of my friends in Nablus and rubber bullets and arrests.

31

AMERICA

I was called into a meeting on base and told that, if I wanted, I could go to America to see the same kids I had toured with around Israel. It was a pilot programme offering the reverse experience of Birthright. The soldiers were being sent over there. I wasn't sure why I was chosen but then again I didn't ask, I just said yes.

My plane landed in Newark airport and I was greeted with grey skies and people with accents straight out of a Martin Scorsese film. I took a train down to Washington, D.C. and then another to College Park Maryland. I flew in with one other soldier and we were scheduled to meet one of the students who had toured with us in Israel. He was going to put us up at his place at College Park. I couldn't remember him at all from the Birthright trip.

The man who organised the programme from the Israeli end was also in College Park and he told me where to be each day and what to do. The nights were mine. The kids from the Birthright trip were all kind of friendly, though decidedly less so than when they were in Israel. Some were happy to see me but others were cold. I imagined they were worried because I had seen all the things they had gotten up to when they were in Israel. Though I couldn't remember much of what had happened.

One day I was told to wear my Class A uniform and red beret. The Israeli organiser drove us along the motorway to a country club in Baltimore. There I was waited on by what appeared to be an exclusively black staff in an all-Jewish country club. I couldn't eat. We were there to meet a rich Jewish guy we were hoping to get money from. He owned an American football team and some other things. My job was to sit there in my IDF uniform and shut the fuck up.

The Israeli organiser was trying to get him to lay out more money to fund this pilot programme I was a part of. Eventually the rich guy started talking about his nephew. I wondered what the relevance was but just sat there and smiled. So did the Israeli guy. He went on to talk about the History Channel. We continued sitting and smiling. Then the man's wife appeared. She listened politely to her husband's rambling for a couple of minutes. He moved on to the World War II battle for Iwo Jima and then American Indians. I couldn't restrain myself any longer and jumped in with a couple of comments about Iwo, but stopped after a receiving a glare from my fellow Israeli. I was a monkey, there to be seen with a red beret and an IDF uniform.

That night I went to a Hillel organised party in Washington, D.C. On the private bus from College Park to the bar I was handed a plastic bottle filled with vodka. I was wasted before I even arrived. I remember being dragged into the bathroom by one of the girls. We were in a cubicle getting friendly but I could hardly stand up. I couldn't remember the girl's name. I tried to look at her but the lights were too bright and I was too drunk to make out her face. And then I knew I was in trouble.

Sometimes you think thoughts without understanding why or being able to control when they burst into the brain. My friends were still roaming around Nablus. They were carrying their rifles and wearing night vision goggles. They were drinking heavy Turkish coffee after every mission and smoking a cigarette before going to sleep, satisfied to still be alive. I was drunk in a bathroom in Washington, D.C., barely able to stand up and kiss a woman whose name I didn't even know. It didn't compute. There were two worlds and I had been granted a temporary excursion from one to the other. But nothing in this other world seemed real.

The next day I was sitting on an intercity bus on my way up to New York City. I passed the journey moving between euphoria and misery as I found myself hungover and ecstatic at the view of the United States outside. It seemed only minutes passed before we hit New York City – that place I had only ever seen in the fantasy of movies and television. When we reached Penn Station I alighted to find a Chassidic Jew removing the bags from the hold.

I had been told that a family had agreed to host me for a couple of nights before my flight back to Israel, and with their address on a piece of paper, I found their apartment in upper Manhattan. An Irish doorman let me into the building. A maid, wearing a black uniform with a white apron let me into the flat. Thankfully I was expected.

She ushered me in and for a moment the two of us stood in the living room staring out of huge windows overlooking the famous Central Park. I met my adopted family and then rushed out to explore the city. The next day was Shabbat and I was under instructions to accompany my adopted family to a nearby shul. It had been stated that I was to attend in my army uniform. The shul was hidden in plain sight, located inside what looked like an apartment building. After the service I was told to give a speech to the congregation thanking them for hosting me. I tried to say something humorous but felt silly standing there in my uniform.

I was shunted off to lunch at a billionaire's home. I didn't understand how I was being moved around from place to place with such ease. There always seemed to be someone connected to the community in charge of what I was doing and where I was going. In fact it seemed like there was an argument going on between my host family and some big shot in the community. The host family wanted me to have Shabbat lunch at their home, whereas the big shot wanted me to go somewhere else. In the end the host family walked off leaving me alone with the big shot who pointed me in the direction of a clique and told me to go with them.

And so I ended up walking into an apartment building that on the outside looked the same as all the others. I moved into the lift with a few of the other guests only to be caught unawares when the doors opened a few floors up. Expecting to enter a hallway it took me a couple of moments to understand I was actually in someone's home. I left the lift and followed everyone else through a house with ceilings that seemed impossibly high for a block of flats. There were golden statuettes of little angels on the walls. The angels hovered over renaissance artwork complete with little brass plaques telling me the name of the artist and the year each piece was painted.

We were shown into a dining room with a long table. I was seated on the far end with about 20 people between me and my host (who hadn't spoken a word to me). A uniformed waiter approached and asked whether I wanted vodka or whisky. I opted for the whisky and asked for a double with ice. The thoughts started again. I remembered trying to sleep in the rain on the top of a hill where all around me was mud. I remembered my first walk through the streets of Nablus and I remembered my friends were far away in that other world called Israel. The man next to me kept talking to me. Sat there in my olive-coloured uniform I felt out of place. I looked at the other people on the table. I was in their world, a world where people had renaissance paintings, and uniformed waiters serving them in their own homes.

The guy next to me was relentless. He had closely cropped hair just when it was on the cusp of being fashionable. His watch was huge. He told me he was done with his years of fucking and doing drugs and was now on a new path as a fashion designer. I didn't know what to say. My mind kept taking itself back to training and operations. I sort of nodded. He kept on. "I'm sorry," I said, "I'm afraid I don't really know anything about fashion, I'm not a very materialistic kind of person." He started talking to me about how he wasn't materialistic at all and that fashion wasn't about being materialistic. I finished my whisky and asked for another. I sat listening, unable to make him stop. There was a mother at the table holding her new born baby who had been handed to her by a maid. I wondered what kind of an adult the baby would become after growing up surrounded by this kind of wealth. I feared the answer was sitting next to me talking about materials and materialism while proclaiming that he had no interest in either.

The man who would become the ambassador to the United States and a member of the Israeli Parliament, Michael Oren, stood up to give a lecture about the Six Day War. He had just published a book on the subject. His lecture was well received. He was sitting near the top of the table and I craned my head to see him. Later he told me his son was serving in the Sayeret of the Nahal brigade. He also told me he had been an officer in my unit during his own service. At the end of his lecture he pointed to me telling the other people there that our unit should have been considered every bit as tough to get into as Harvard or Yale. I think I blushed. Then the white-haired host gestured to someone else around the table. It was Elie Wiesel the Nobel Peace Prize Laureate. I had read a couple of his books but hadn't known what he looked like. My jaw dropped. Where was I again?

Wiesel simply nodded slowly to acknowledge the host's introduction. He was there with his wife. She was blonde and had been speaking French for the duration of the meal. I didn't hear Wiesel speak a word the whole time I was there. I found it difficult to comprehend that he was in the room and even if I had he was too far away from me to speak to him. Were these people really there I wondered or maybe they were there and I was somewhere else?

I remember nothing of the food. I just remember some kind

of resistance kicking in. The thought that the world shouldn't be this good bounced around in my mind. There was a place in this world where people lived with golden angels and classical paintings on their walls and where uniformed staff served them their food and maids took the baby for you whenever you wanted.

I ended up taking the lift down with Wiesel. I studied his face up close. I had read his book *Legends of Our Time*. There was a chapter where he describes coming face-to-face with his kapo from Auschwitz on a Jerusalem bus. He stays on the bus long past his stop. He can't leave because he sees this man and is fixated on him. He gets off where his kapo gets off to confront him. The kapo starts shouting at him in German and Wiesel runs away from him. I was left wondering if this ever happened, or if this was how he imagined the confrontation would be. I had grown up on stories about the Holocaust. Every Jew had. It embedded itself into the Jewish psyche, giving all of us survivor's guilt whether we were related to someone who suffered through it or not. Seeing him made my service more poignant. I was a Jew in the 21st century. I held a rifle and wore a uniform and made the phrase "Never again" a fact rather than a slogan.

Wiesel came from a dead Jewish world I'll never know and he seemed to have one foot firmly planted in it. As the lift descended I stood there gawping at him, trying to think of something to say. I wanted to tell him that I was one of the new Jews; I was a Jew with a rifle, a Jew who held his head up high with pride. I wanted to tell him that he need not worry, that we had risen from the ashes reborn with our own country and held power in our hands. I said nothing. I just looked at him until the lift hit the ground floor. And then I left New York and the USA for Israel.

32

The Girl

While I had been in the USA the unit had been posted to the Jenin area of operations. Rather than sending everyone to a military base, the unit was posted to a kibbutz in the North of Israel. It was to this kibbutz I made my way. For the past week I'd been worried about my friends. The relief of knowing that nothing had happened to any of them was like a powerful drug allowing me to return to the army far more at ease than the state I had been in while away. Added to that was the excitement of knowing we would be going out on ops in Jenin.

During Operation Defensive Shield Jenin had been the scene of heavy fighting which saw the deaths of a number of boys from Golani. The terrorists there had earned the city a reputation as being the toughest in the West Bank alongside Nablus. Getting to operate in Jenin was like playing in the cup final.

One operation stands out. It started when Motti walked into our room and told us we had a briefing in the kibbutz bomb shelter (our makeshift briefing room) and that it was starting in two minutes. I grabbed my rifle and followed the others there. The Major was away inspecting the rookies, so Black was in charge.

A projector had been set up in the centre of the room on a table. An aerial photograph of the target was projected onto a wall. It wasn't to be Jenin but a village nearby. Dust and cigarette smoke rose and swirled in the beam of the projector reminding me of the briefings that I had seen in old war movies. Covering the rest of the table was a collection of maps of the area, some small scale some large.

Black started his briefing with a sigh. We were going to an isolated village to pick up a suicide bomber. According to intelligence the bomber had no bodyguards so no resistance was anticipated. I took a look at the maps and saw that the path to the house was easy to remember as there were no houses or alleyways next to it. No problems anticipated.

The journey to the village took forever. We sat squashed in the vehicle with everyone sitting on top of each other and equipment all over the place. It was pitch black as there were no windows in the back of the vehicle. I tried to sleep but I was too uncomfortable. No one even tried to speak over the sound of the diesel engine. Despite trying not to, I concentrated on what could go wrong and whether it was a good idea to send just ten of us to an isolated village in the middle of the night. The more I thought about it the more it sounded like the plot of a bad horror movie.

The vehicle lumbered up to its destination and we gratefully tumbled out of it and sorted ourselves out into a straight line, with Black at the front. It was so dark I could hardly see the man in front of me. The house we were sneaking our way towards was the only building I could see. I tried looking for the rest of the village through my night scope but saw nothing. The grass on the ground was long and reached up past my ankles. It felt like Mother Nature herself was giving me resistance. I wondered if the resistance was a prelude to gunfire, a warning perhaps to get out while I still could. There were some white lights behind me and off to my left. I assumed that they were illuminating other houses but in the darkness all I could see was a mere twinkle of white light, like a distant star, shining at eye level. I longed to see a bright, beaming moon high up in the sky illuminating anyone that may have been waiting to ambush us in the long grass. Yet there was no moon to be found, only clouds in the black night sky.

We soon came upon the target house, standing alone with a

dilapidated stone wall running around it. We divided into two teams of five – I took up a covering position in front of the house as Black and his team moved towards the door. I placed my rifle on top of the wall and searched through the view finder for anything out of the ordinary. We watched Black move his team towards the house and bang on the door until he received a response from the unseen people inside.

The green metal door creaked open and a woman appeared. When she saw Black she immediately started shrieking. Then the rest of the family poured out of the house after her. Now there were nine of them standing there but no girl. After Black said a few words to them, the mother moved inside to fetch her daughter. As the mother brought out her daughter, the family instinctively stood silently in a protective semi-circle around her. The mother was fat, the daughter was thin, the mother was olive skinned the daughter light skinned, the mother wore a hijab, her daughter didn't. She was a tall, slender girl who stood with her head bowed, strands of red hair covering her face.

I wondered how she felt at that moment. Did she really intend to blow herself up? Or had she simply been full of bravado, joining a terrorist group without understanding the commitment she had made? It must have been easy for her to talk about blowing herself up when surrounded by supporters, but what about now, with the consequences of her actions turning up on her doorstep to cart her away? I didn't even know what happened to the people that we arrested. I couldn't help but wonder how this girl was going to be able to cope with an interrogation by a seasoned intelligence operative. How long would it take for him to find the chinks in her emotional armour? How long before she cracked and gave up the names of her associates? Probably not very long.

Once Black confirmed we had the right girl someone blindfolded and handcuffed her. When it was time to leave the mother wailed and shrieked only to be restrained by a man I assumed was her husband. She lunged for Black's rifle and actually got a hand on it. For that act he probably could have shot her right there according to our rules of engagement. He didn't, though he looked like he was going to hit her. He didn't do that either. While the exchange was taking place the daughter was already being bundled off, the family impotent to do anything about it. We weren't going to leave the girl there because of her mother's complaints. It was unusual though; most of the time the family simply hung their heads in silence, too much in shock to move or resist. Perhaps it was different this time because we were arresting a 17-year-old girl. With our objective achieved we pulled out leaving the family standing at their front door.

She said nothing as we put her in the car and drove away. A few minutes into the journey the tears started to pour down her face. I watched her, at first dispassionately, but after a while I felt sorry for her – this girl with milky white skin and a shock of lovely long, red hair. As we drove back I constructed an imaginary story for how she had ended up in an Israeli army vehicle on her way to prison. It's amazing the extent to which tears can convince you that someone is innocent – this girl who wanted to blow herself up.

Her tears flowed, but her whimpering was quiet, allowing me to rest my head on the side of the vehicle, close my eyes and get some sleep. The vehicle trundled on with a squad of commandoes and a wannabe suicide bomber all locked into a cramped space together with no windows and no idea where we were going.

We arrived at our destination; a military prison, more like a holding base where the prisoners were placed temporarily and processed into the system. Someone took the girl out of the car and into the base. The guard there wouldn't allow our vehicle in so we had to park outside. Someone shook me out of my half-sleep and I emerged into the morning light blinking, watching from afar as the blindfolded, handcuffed girl was led into the army base. I took the pack of cigarettes from my shirt pocket, put one in my mouth and lit it. I inhaled the smoke deep into my lungs. My watch said 06:55 and I was enjoying my first cigarette of the day, thinking about how wonderful it would be to finally get back to the kibbutz and bed. Black wasn't there; he had ridden in a jeep and had gone off somewhere either to catch some sleep or to brief the higher ups. That meant Motti was in charge of us, and the girl.

I took my final drag and moved towards the metal gate of the prison. No one protested my entry inside and I quickly found Motti. He was standing in a courtyard arguing with someone from the base. Standing off to the side and alone was the girl. She wasn't crying but had clearly just finished. Still blindfolded and still cuffed, it seemed no one knew what to do with her.

I moved towards her placing my hand on the knife that I kept in my combat vest. No one noticed me as I moved up to her and cut her plasticuffs with one short sharp tug. She groaned and immediately grabbed her wrists. Whoever had put the cuffs on her had tied them too tightly and almost cut her circulation. She had deep, red lines on her wrist where the cuffs had been. I put the straw from my drinking bag in her mouth and allowed her to drink deeply. She was still blindfolded.

I placed my hand on her shoulder gesturing for her to sit down and then put new cuffs on her. Not able to think of anything else to do for her I moved away and walked straight into the rest of the guys. There was a problem, the prison was full and they protested that there was nowhere to put the girl. Since no officers had accompanied us to the base there was no one with enough seniority to force a resolution.

I listened in to the increasingly irate argument over the girl. I hated non-combat soldiers. They're called jobnikim and they sit in their air conditioned offices, breezing through their military service while we combat soldiers did all the work. They hated us too, they considered us to be idiots. Usually there wasn't a problem, as we were kept apart by our different roles, but on that morning we clashed. "What do you expect us to do with her?" Motti screamed at a lanky guard.

It was too early in the morning for me to be bothered to get involved and I walked away. Sometimes low rank has its benefits. It was incredible to me that after risking life and limb to pick up a suicide bomber we should have to fight harder against the bureaucracy of our own side than against the Palestinians. A major drove into the base. At first the guard on the gate refused to admit him but changed his mind once the officer started shouting at him. The power of rank.

I lit up another cigarette. Several of the other guys joined me. All of us were resigned to the army's bureaucracy and the fact there was nothing any of us could do about it. Now that we were back in Israel proper, it didn't seem to matter all that much anyway.

Motti tired of arguing with the soldier. There were no officers there from our own unit to back him up. Technically she was our responsibility. The guards had refused to fill out the necessary paperwork. By now all of us had been awake for over 24 hours – all of us, that is, except the jailer. He carried on talking about his idea to tie the girl to the fence and in a few hours when a prisoner was moved they would put her in the vacated cell. I could see Motti's resolve crack especially when the others started complaining about still being at the base.

I knew that we shouldn't do it, but at the same time I didn't care that much if we did. The guys were right; why should we treat a terrorist like anything other than a terrorist? The longer things dragged on and the more tired I became the less I cared. Enough was enough. After being unable to contact any of our own officers and with no other way out in sight, he took out some more cuffs and shackled the girl to the fence. We jumped into the car and set off towards the kibbutz to rest.

I think about her sometimes, wondering what happened to

her: the 17-year-old who wanted to be remembered forever as a martyr. How many lives had we saved when we picked her up? The one we left shackled to the fence like a wild animal, hunted down but not caged. I wonder if we had been as she imagined us to be, if she had expected better or worse from us, or if she even cared. A few days later the deputy commander of the unit walked into our room, "That girl on the fence – not good … an officer will accompany you to the jail in the future." And that was that. He couldn't say anything else because he knew an officer should have accompanied us then too.

33

DYING AND KILLING IN NABLUS

Mines and booby traps were enjoying a period of great success when we rotated back to Nablus. The guys we replaced were from the Nahal Brigade and we felt they hadn't been carrying out enough operations to stop terrorist activity. We were going to have to carry out some tough operations to end what had become regular instances of these devices exploding on our troops.

We went out on our first op the night we rotated back in. We were sent to two different addresses in the kasbah looking for the same terrorist. With all the mines blowing up none of us thought we would make it to the targets. The upswing in violence in the Nablus area was reflected in Jerusalem and Tel Aviv where suicide bombers had killed dozens and wounded hundreds.

It was the same but it was different. The vehicles were the same, the people with me were the same but we were all sure something was going to happen to us that night. No one spoke about it but the feeling showed itself in every word that wasn't spoken and in the times we made eye contact with one another during the briefing. I could feel it coming from everyone. Only the night before a mine had exploded on a Nahal patrol. A couple of days before that an officer had been killed by a mine.

I can't remember who suggested it but as the vehicle trundled its way toward our objective we all closed together until we were locked in a group hug, helmet to helmet, rifles on our laps while Forrest read out the prayer for the wellbeing of soldiers. I had the prayer laminated and took it into every mission with me. My mum had bought it for me in Jerusalem and I took it out and handed it to Forrest so he could read the blessing out. I looked at each of my friends in turn as he did so, certain one of us wouldn't make it back.

The vehicle stopped and we broke out of it. The second team was just ahead of us. The other team moved first. Once we had formed up we started moving. I remember turning and looking at Forrest who was in front of me and to my left. He winked at me.

Then he disappeared. Consumed by white light.

I saw the flash first, then I heard the bang. At first I thought someone had dropped a stun grenade by mistake but the light was too intense. I seemed to be trapped in it. I couldn't see anything around me save for white light. The world went fuzzy and white; the alleyway was gone, the guys who had been all around me were gone. It was just me. And I understood.

This was death.

It wasn't bad at all. No pain and gone in an instant. I couldn't help but wonder how it was that they were right about the all-encompassing white light. A high-pitched tone permeated my skull. The white light now shone down from above me. Around me was a white fog.

Then I heard voices, "Oren ok," "Liran ok," "Uzi ok," then I heard my voice saying, "Marc ok." The white light shone down at me through the haze. The silhouettes of my friends emerged. Those poor fools I thought. Checking in as though we're all still alive. But I had checked in with them.

I patted my body down searching for blood, exactly as I had been trained. When I didn't find any it was further proof I was dead. It couldn't be that I was unscathed after such a blast. But the dust literally began to settle. I looked up at the white light to see a lamp post. A cloud of dust had enveloped the world around me. The white neon light bounced off the dust. Everything looked white. Forrest had activated a booby trap, which was attached to a door. The force had thrown him to the ground. So he got up. When trying to figure it all out later we imagined that the builder of the device had put it together without including ball bearings or any other shrapnel. It was about ten minutes since we'd prayed together.

The order came from the various radios carried by different commanders. "Continue as planned." The voice came through static in that classic radio squawk. I wanted to get out of there and go home. But no one asked me. The officer commanding the other team thought he could see another IED waiting for us down an alleyway. He threw a grenade but didn't detonate it. He threw another. It still didn't blow up.

Amit called everyone back to the vehicles. He sent my team to a building overlooking our position. It already had a recon team of four guys inserted. They had seen movement on a rooftop between our position and theirs. He sent the other team back into their armoured car and told the driver to keep revving the engine as if the car was going to move forward. Our armoured car gunned it to the building and we stormed up the steps to the roof. Adrenaline carried me up. Security went to the wind as we rushed to the top to join the recon team. I grinned at one of them who said to me, "You think you had it bad? I had to watch you all go up in smoke!"

Motti spread us along the roof and spotted three guys lying on the rooftop between our new position and the alleyway we'd been in minutes before. They had positioned themselves to fire down on us in an ambush. I couldn't see them. Everyone else had them. The recon team leader was watching them through a thermal optic device and was practically having kittens. Motti told us to use three bullets each. I still couldn't see the terrorists and whispered as much to him. Motti lit them up with an infrared laser beam only someone with night vision goggles can see. I saw the beam through my scope. I aimed at it but still couldn't see anyone. Motti started the count that ended with the word "fire".

As one we opened up. No one stopped after three rounds. When we switched magazines the commander of the recon team shouted at us, "They're still alive, one's moving for the door!" So we opened up on them again. I blind fired at the roof. This time he reported they were all still. I felt nothing while firing; I couldn't even see anyone. I might as well have been at the range, except at the range I could see my target. The rest of the night was spent directing the other team to the relevant roof to recover the bodies. The kasbah was such a maze of homes and dwellings built ramshackle on top of each other that they couldn't get to the right rooftop. The call to prayer was made from the mosques signalling the time to leave. Daylight was on the way and cars would soon be moving for the checkpoints. I guess Amit decided there had been enough action for one night and we pulled out. I thought of that night in Jenin when I had wanted to throttle the sniper. I thought that maybe the same thing had happened to me, that the targets had been right there and that something was happening inside my head that refused to allow me to see them.

34

MY KIDS!

We had one minute to get into position. After a minute the unit would move regardless of whether we were covering them. Speed was the key. One magic minute after we left the vehicle the other guys were going in. Speed and surprise were everything.

The armoured car stopped and my sergeant, said the magic word "PRIKA", I kicked open the back doors of the Knight armoured vehicle and eight of us ran out. To keep count of the time I used a technique taught during training. I imagined a metronome ticking down the seconds – every time the metronome in my head moved from one side to another I shifted my rifle to cover a slightly different angle while counting down another second.

We reached the door of the apartment building and proceeded up the stairs.

43 seconds left.

I was third in line and taking pains to keep the barrel of my rifle in a relevant direction as we climbed.

38 seconds left.

The lights in the building were dim as we clattered our way up ever higher. The metronome kept ticking. I kept adjusting my rifle while on the move.

31 seconds left

We were at the apartment door.

The first in line was covering the stairs that continued up to the next floor, the last was pointing his rifle down in the direction from which we've come. I was banging on the apartment door.

"OPEN, OPEN, OPEN, OPEN, OPEN THE FUCKING DOOR!"

30 seconds.

The door wasn't opening and I'd taken to kicking the steel and pounding on it with my fists. It was past 2 a.m. Whoever was inside needed to open the door or Uzi and Liran and all my best friends were going to be running into a potential trap. The metronome was ticking down. I was shouting frantically at the closed door. I had a pack on my back with a sledgehammer and crowbar in it but if I had to use those tools we were going to be late.

20 seconds.

I heard a bolt slide on the other side. A man opened the door a fraction. I could hear him saying something about "yeladim, yeladim" the Hebrew word for children. I wasn't interested in children; I was interested in a window and I knew exactly where it was.

15 seconds.

I shoulder-barged into the door and we all piled in. I charged forward towards a closed door that was the gateway to my window. I could hear the sergeant behind me reasoning with the man who was vainly pleading "shhhh yeladim sheli". I knew the flat from the briefing; everything was where it was supposed to be.

12 seconds left. I was going to make it in time.

I kicked the door open and stepped in, rifle at the ready. There was a woman lying in bed propped up on an elbow with a confused look on her face. "Get up! Get out!" I said but she just kept staring at me. Her sleep disturbed, she looked at me standing there in her doorway. I was going to say something else but the words stuck in my throat. She didn't look afraid or even angry, just confused as if I was the dinner guest she forgot she invited.

My eyes flickered away from the figure in the white nightgown to the window – my window. The metronome kept ticking while I stood there. It ticked down to zero but I couldn't move, nor could I speak. I had lost my voice.

Standing there, sweat trickling into my eyes I knew the truth. I was a terrible soldier. I should have pulled her out of her bed, smashed the glass of the window and stood there with my rifle trained on the outside covering my friends while they went to take out the terrorists from the building opposite. Instead I had betrayed them, left them to go into harm's way without my help. I felt my Sergeant's hand on my shoulder. "Give her a couple of minutes to get herself together."

I stared dumbfounded at the half-naked woman and slowly stepped backwards towards the door. All the momentum gone, all the adrenaline evaporated. I could still hear her husband pleading with the other guys "my kids, my kids." A couple of minutes later the woman stepped out of the room all clad in black and wearing her headscarf. I escorted her, together with her two toddlers, towards the front door. Her husband had already been sent upstairs to let his neighbours know that they would be staying with them for the night. Two members of my squad stood at another window opened fire without warning just as we were walking behind them.

The woman screamed in panic, her two kids started crying. I don't know what has caused the guys to start shooting. I motioned the civilians down into the corner that offered the most protection, while waiting for the shooting to stop. Once it was safe they left the front door for another apartment upstairs and I didn't see them again for the rest of the operation.

After an intense start the operation dragged on for days. Intelligence insisted there were some of their most wanted terrorists holed up in the building opposite the apartment we had taken over. We provided cover while the building was searched once, twice, three times. They brought in dogs to search the place. It was my turn at watch. I was standing at the window the guys fired from on the first night. There was nothing to shoot at now.

There was nothing to shoot at the night before either. Just two soldiers ordered to open fire at the walls of the building to scare anyone inside and make them think twice about making a run for it. I was looking at the dog being held in place by his handler. He was a beautiful German Shepherd but something was wrong with him. He leaped up at his handler barking, then he went for an officer of the Sayeret, then he started chasing his tail. The officer put a bullet in the dog's brain. The handler knelt to the ground running his hand over the dog's coat as we watched from above.

35

GUARDING THE FORTRESS

Rumours swept through the unit about a month before the official word came down. Naturally it was Uzi who found out first and let us know that we were being sent into the line. Line duty can only be described as occupation duty. You man the checkpoints and the watchtowers, and sit in the jeeps making mobile patrols throughout the West Bank. It's the opposite philosophy to operations. When we were operating previously the enemy never knew when we were coming, giving us the advantage. That advantage didn't exist when manning static checkpoints or watchtowers that couldn't move.

Line duty had no end: you worked your shift and then you waited for the next one. It would also involve dealing with Palestinians as a matter of course. On operations you deal with civilians only as a part of achieving a stated objective. Usually if civilians were there it was because they had gotten in the way somehow. With line duty Palestinian civilians were part and parcel of the work.

That's why line duty is simultaneously the most dangerous, boring and soul-destroying task a soldier can be given. It is the mainstay of the work that regular infantry and tank battalions have to cope with and the main reason soldiers volunteer for special units. They'll force themselves to go through the toughest training the IDF has just to avoid the stress and boredom of line duty. Now, after all the training and nights spent wandering around Palestinian towns we were going to do line duty anyway.

We were assigned to guard a small settlement near Nablus

called Migdalim. We were to be there for four months. The settlement was on top of a hill. A small Palestinian town, Kutsra was located at the foot of the hill. In addition to guarding Migdalim we were to patrol the surrounding area in jeeps and Humvees.

The first thing I noticed about the settlement was the number of empty houses. I wasn't surprised and found it difficult to imagine why anyone would want to live there while the Intifada raged around them. Someone had given permission for those houses to be built and people may well have bought them but they sat empty and unfinished. It made me think of the constant news reports about new settlement units being built and the diplomatic controversy around them. To see the empty houses standing there made the whole thing feel like a con. The government announced new houses to be built, then built them only to have them standing empty and incomplete. Then they sent soldiers in to guard them.

There were two watchtowers in Migdalim. To reach one of them we'd always have to walk past a row of empty properties. I rarely saw any of the residents of the settlement, except for the local settlement security guy. An overweight, balding man around 60 years old, he always swaggered around with a short M16 slung over his shoulder. He occasionally barked orders at us. We tended to be polite but ignored his instructions.

I participated in my first jeep patrol between four in the morning and twelve in the afternoon. We drove up and down a road for eight hours in an armoured Humvee. It was to prove a pattern of the next few months. During these jeep patrols boredom assumed a new meaning. We drove up and down the main road, as well as around the dirt tracks that connected the nearby towns and villages. It was these dirt tracks that contained the real traffic as they allowed the locals to avoid checkpoints. So we spent most of our time driving around on these dirt tracks.

Sometimes we'd set up a temporary roadblock. We'd park the

Humvee or jeep and stop traffic on the pathway and then let each vehicle through one at a time after asking the driver a couple of questions and checking the occupant's ID. It was impossible to know who was lying, who was dangerous and who was neither. We looked at the car a little but if we had searched each car thoroughly we wouldn't have had time to patrol anywhere during the shift. So we made cursory inspections of everything ensuring that terrorists knew that there were no safe routes for them.

Kutsra was the closest Palestinian town to Migdalim so we'd spend more time moving through there than almost anywhere else. Sometimes the kids there would throw stones at us when we drove through. Most of the time we'd drive in there hoping they would so that we could have a break from eight hours cooped up in a jeep in the heat of summer.

Just driving into the village was a provocation for the people who lived there. We knew that, but our duties were to patrol the village anyway so that didn't really matter. We moved through there as often as we could. If we were bored we would convince whoever the commander was to drive all around the village in the hope that someone would throw a stone, giving us the excuse to break out the anti-riot gear.

At the entrance to the village there was a large plot of land upon which were the wrecks of dozens of cars. Many had Israeli licence plates on them. The rumour was that these car wrecks represented the best instance of Israeli–Palestinian cooperation the region had ever known. Car thieves in Israel would steal vehicles on one side of the Green Line and then sell them on the other. The valuable vehicles would then be driven into Jordan and shipped off to a client paying top dollar. The ones that weren't valuable ended up rotting in a village like Kutsra. The army ran things on the Palestinian side of the Green Line and we were interested in catching terrorists not car thieves. By selling to Palestinians the Israeli criminals ensured they were less likely to get caught since there were fewer police around to run plates or chase after them.

On moving further inside the village on the main road you could carry on driving straight, which would take you past the school, or turn left up a steep hill into the most populous part of the village. If you were to turn left and move about ten metres up the hill you would arrive at the main junction. It was at this junction that the kids would really pelt stones at us. Some days we drove in just in time for the end of the school day and so they were all there to greet us. The sound of stones hitting the car was the indicator of a mini battle beginning and welcome respite from sitting doing nothing in the car. It was the same principle as hide and seek. They'd throw things at us and then run and hide, waiting for an opening when no one could see before peeking out to throw more stones or bottles. For our part, we had stun grenades and gas grenades and an intense desire to leap out of the vehicles. Live rounds were fired at a wall if things got too intense. This signified a timeout.

The first time I left the vehicle in this situation was to throw a gas grenade at a group of stone throwers hiding behind a wall. They were kids between the ages of 5 up to about 12 or 13. They were throwing everything they could get their hands on from rocks and stones to glass bottles. I remember the silence that descended as I left the safety of the vehicle. Everything slowed down. I felt one of the stones hit my helmet and bounce off.

I saw, for the first time, the young men smoking their sheeshas in the cafe by the junction. There was an older moustachioed man standing on the shop floor staring at me. I saw veiled women looking at me from the windows of the mass of square homes that had been built on the hill. I saw their washing hanging from lines on the roofs and balconies and I heard the chuckles of kids as they hid from me in the nearest alleyway. A soft voice at my ear startled me: "Is there is a problem?" I spun around to see a slight man with a moustache. He stood there, an oasis of calm amidst the play violence between us soldiers and the youth of his village. By his calm demeanour in the middle of the ruckus he had exposed the nonsense for what it was. He could walk around without fear of anything hitting him because he knew that this was a game strictly between the school kids and the soldiers. It's also why the older teens could sit smoking their sheeshas. They'd already been through this phase and moved on. I'd already pulled the pin on a gas grenade but I looked at this man astonished before throwing it over a wall at the stonethrowers.

I watched 20 kids run shouting from the alleyway up the hill to continue their miniature assault from high ground. My officer shouted for me to get back into the jeep. "Don't get out of the vehicle like that again," he admonished me.

"It was a good throw though," I countered. He had to agree that the grenade had hit in just the right place. Then he ordered the driver to turn us around and continue up to the next village. The driver told me the man who spoke to me was the Mukhtar of the village.

At first, all such contacts were exciting and offered a feeling of meaning to the long, drawn-out patrols that covered asphalt main roads and dirt tracks through villages. This waned quickly, however. The excitement and adrenaline that necessarily comes from having things thrown at you didn't survive my first close quarters contact with the enemy.

We were driving through Kutsra and the outbreak of hostilities was signalled by a clump of mud and rock hitting the grating over my open window. We opened our doors and burst out as one to throw stun grenades. Our driver shouted, "There's one!" I jumped back into the vehicle as he pushed his foot on the accelerator and we stormed forward. The burst of speed had sent a group of kids charging in the other direction but one hadn't been paying attention and had been left behind. The driver kicked open his door and seized the kid's arm shouting a triumphant "aha!"

I looked at the driver's prize. He was a child of about 5 years old. He started crying. The driver, Assim, was oblivious. "Let's take him to the police station," he said. I looked at this kid, deserted by his friends now standing 100m away watching. Throwing gas and stun grenades at these children from a distance was easy enough but looking at this kid close up was different.

"Let him go," I said to Assim. He looked over his shoulder at me distraught that his prize was going to be allowed to go free.

"If we take him to the police station he'll think twice before throwing stones at us again," he protested.

"Just fucking let him go," I retorted and was relieved to see Assim release his grip. The tears disappeared and the kid ran off happily to re-join his friends and get back into the fight. This is what it had come to: Marc Goldberg of Orev Tzanhanim versus the 5-year-old from Kutsra. My enthusiasm for the activity waned.

36

KIBBUTZ

Before Migdalim we had been based on the Israeli side of the Green Line. Each night we had moved out by bus to the nearest base from where we'd move into Nablus to carry out our mission. Sometimes we'd rotate and spend a few weeks on an army base next to Nablus and move straight from there to our operations. Line duty changed that. We were there all the time and would guard during the day and carry out operations at night. It was hard to get to grips with the fact that at seven in the morning on a Friday I could be covering friends on the streets of Nablus and by twelve in the afternoon I could be sitting in a bar by Tel Aviv beach. The area of fighting and "home" were so close to one another and so utterly different from each other that it was confusing to make the transition from danger to safety. I couldn't remember which of the two places was home?

At this point in my service the lease on my Tel Aviv apartment came to an end. Someone on my team from a kibbutz not far from Haifa suggested I move there. I agreed and made the move. My friend's family welcomed me warmly and sorted me out a room on the kibbutz. Around the same time, operations stepped up in the West Bank.

The bus back to the kibbutz became a portal to another planet – a magical tour bus transporting me from a world of darkness and pain to a place of sunshine, hope and happiness. But the difference was chaotic on my mind. Slowly I retreated from the world around me when I was released. My friend's parents had invited me to Friday night dinners with them whenever I was out. At first I went but after a while I couldn't face this jovial family atmosphere. When my friend was there I would hang out with his kibbutz friends but slowly I retreated from them too.

I didn't know exactly why it was that I couldn't handle being around "normal" people anymore. I just knew I couldn't. So I retired to my room each and every time I returned from the army, locking the door and resting my rifle in the corner, where I could always see it. I remember sitting on my bed waiting to go back into the army. I also remember coming back and simply sitting in the shower until the hot water ran out, just sitting, thinking about the week or weeks that had gone before, of the people I had seen and the operations I had carried out.

One of the guys on the kibbutz was in a recon unit for one of the tank brigades. He'd made a drug bust somewhere in the desert. They'd stopped a guy carrying a mountain of hashish and helped themselves to as much as they could. He brought home a brick of the stuff. One day he broke off a chunk and handed it to me. That was it, they never saw me again. I lay in bed every time I returned and smoked myself into oblivion. If I left the room it was for supplies. With furtive glances to the left and right I'd run over to the kibbutz mini market to pick up food for the weekend, then head back to my room and lock the door.

I wondered what they were saying about me, the lone soldier who rarely left his room and when he did was in a drug-induced stupor. It made it even harder to leave. The invitations to dinner never stopped coming but I never felt comfortable accepting them. I never really felt comfortable on the kibbutz, I never knew what to say to people or how to behave. I just wanted to be in my room the whole time. There was a pub on the kibbutz – I remember going there one night and actually pretending to be stoned in the hope no one there would talk to me.

The hashish never relieved my unease it just softened the dull ache of the tension caused by the ambushes and arrests. The knowledge that I would be doing them again when I went back ensured I was particularly loath to get used to being away from the army. Why get used to being away only to have to go straight back? Snapshots of the previous missions ran through my mind. They all jumbled on top of each other, my first missions and my most recent ones all fell in on each other creating a collage of memories without chronology. In my mind's eye I always returned to the old woman sitting on her steps in the courtyard in the Old City of Nablus. The home with the kid kicking a ball to me and the man carrying his colostomy bag with a look of pain on his face. And the old woman looking at me; pleading with me with her eyes.

At the same time I lamented the lack of action. Before the army I had visions of battlefields and glory, yet all I had found was filth. The stink of it everywhere, filth on the streets from the garbage, the smell of shit that greeted my nostrils on every foray into the towns and villages, the filthy work that we were doing. And back to the pleading black eyes of the old woman. I felt no remorse; I wasn't apologetic for searching through her home or those of others. When I saw her in my mind's eye I felt the same way I had felt that first time I saw her: distant, disconnected. I wondered what she expected of me with her pleading eyes? Had she not seen countless numbers of soldiers traipse though her home? So why me? Why did she choose to sear herself into my consciousness?

My sleep pattern deteriorated when I left the army to go "home". I lay awake on that foam mattress trying to make some sense out of my life. How could the army become a career for me now? I had wanted to go all the way to the top, to become a general and then on to politics as so many other generals had. But how could I stand it now? How could I do it off the back of all this? My heart and soul cried out for battle but there seemed to be no battles left to fight. The Temple Mount had been liberated, the Six Day War fought and won. Yoni Netanyahu, the solider who rescued the hostages at Entebbe airport and commander of the most elite Special Forces unit Sayeret Matkal, was long dead. Meir Har-Zion the famous paratrooper hero of the 1950s and 60s was just an angry old man. The Paratroopers had jumped into combat just once, long before I was born.

The glory had already been stolen by those who came before me. I was a warrior born into the wrong age. There was no raid on Entebbe for me, just an unending number of Palestinian homes to rummage through, suicide bombers on the streets of Israel and eight-hour-long vehicle patrols to wind up school kids. Yoni Netanyahu was dead and I was all that was left.

I started taking pointless risks. One night I was back from the army and had hitchhiked to the kibbutz. My ride had taken me as far as a lonely junction about ten minutes' drive from my foam mattress and my hashish. There had been a warning that terrorists were on the lookout in the area for soldiers to kidnap. I stood on the junction in my uniform, red beret on my shoulder, and with my weapon locked and loaded. My thumb sat on the safety switch hoping for the opportunity to use it. I wanted a car to come by with terrorists who would try to kidnap me. I stood willing them to come so I could kill them. If I couldn't find the war in Nablus then I would find it in Israel proper.

Cars drove by but none stopped. It didn't bother me, I was hoping the enemy would find me and then we could fight properly, the way soldiers were supposed to. Without civilians to get shot in the crossfire, without searching through homes, without rubber bullets and without enemies I shot at but couldn't see. Eventually an army jeep came by and stopped to pick me up. The officer driving couldn't believe I had been there all alone, "Are you crazy!" he exclaimed rather than asked, "Man, the enemy would just love to kidnap a soldier!"

He was a junior lieutenant and I was ashamed to hear his words. I silently raged in the back seat that an officer in the IDF could allow himself to be so afraid. I wore the uniform, I had the red beret: let the other guy fear me! I sat there silently but a sneer crept across my face. He dropped me off at the entrance to the kibbutz. I only emptied my weapon of the round in the chamber and the magazine after I had locked the door of my room behind me. I placed it in the corner where it always sat, then I lay on the bed and lamented the fact that the enemy hadn't shown up.

There was no turning point for me, no one instance that had made me this way, just a year of training for a war that I wasn't fighting. The funny thing with all of this going on in my head was that I loved being in the army even more during my time on kibbutz. It got to the point where I hated being away from army life. Away from the army there were only more long, hash-fuelled nights of solitude and thinking too much. I wanted to do more and more operations. I wanted to go out on every op I could just in case a chance for combat lay beyond the fence of the base.

37

PEACE WITH SWEETS

My crew managed to get a new officer, a blond kid called Levine. The first time I spent any time with him was on an eight-hour jeep patrol. I met him and Forrest by the old jeep we would be taking. As usual, Assim the driver wasn't yet ready and so we waited outside his cabin for him. Levine turned to me and said, "Marc, since he's taking so long, why don't you run off to the kitchen and grab us breakfast?" I moved off towards the kitchen and opened the fridge. It was the beginning of the month and so the cooks had splashed out on cheeses and yoghurt, as well as bags of chocolate milk. I grabbed as much as I could carry and moved back to the jeep to find Assim had finally got himself out of bed and was putting on his body armour.

We headed off towards the local villages. On the way into Kutsra this time all I could see was the 5-year-old crying over and over again. The predictability of the situation made me feel like we had all been sucked into a vortex where we were fated to constantly behave the same way, regardless of whether we wanted to. It didn't really matter whether we wanted to go into Kutsra or not. It didn't really matter whether we got off on the violence or not. The town was in our area of responsibility so we had to patrol through it regardless.

We were in one of the old jeeps not a Humvee. Forrest and I sat facing each other with a small double door between us as once again our jeep rolled into Kutsra. When we wanted to deploy one of us would kick the door open and jump out the back. This time I kicked the rear door open and instead of throwing a stun grenade or pointing my rifle at anyone I waved and smiled. We were on the outskirts of the town just moving past the car lot and there was one kid walking there behind us. He saw my smile and his mouth simply dropped. I tried the only non-swear words I know in Arabic. "Kif halek" (meaning how's it going?), I shouted at him and waved. He just stood there with his jaw open for a moment before waving back at me.

I raided Forrest's snack box and threw the biscuits one by one at kids we drove past on the way into town. If they looked at me I smiled and waved at them shouting "kif halek?". As we progressed further in, I left the door open and continued waving and smiling to the people that I saw. Forrest did too and before long we were throwing biscuits and sweets out of the jeep to people. I told the driver to pull over at the main crossroads in the town, something that appeared to unnerve Levine sitting in the front, though he didn't say anything. I hadn't realised just how many kids there were in the village until I saw about 50 of them standing just behind the jeep facing me and Forrest. I left the jeep and gave out the last couple of wafers. Then we just seemed to look at each other for a while without having a clue what to do next.

I was about to try saying something when a 10-year-old kid, dressed in a V-neck sweater and shirt buttoned all the way up to the collar, stepped forward and pointed at himself saying "Hassan". I pointed to my body armour saying "Marc". The kids all started giggling and I was inundated by a chorus of kids pointing at themselves and shouting out their names. I saw that the older guys, about my age, were sitting holding their sheesha pipes looking at the crazy soldier and the crazy kids talking to each other. I wanted to make the moment continue for as long as I could. I'd got away from that vortex of conflict that felt so all encompassing. The kids started talking to me, and talking to each other as though there were no conflict, no bullshit.

Eventually Levine told me to get in the car and I obeyed. I

figured I'd taken the 'Marc Goldberg Accords' as far as they were going to go that day. Perhaps from now on when I returned to the town we would be able to play the scene again for the others and something positive might emerge from it. Once back in the car we moved on down the dusty track towards the next village. On the way I thought about my experiment. I had broken a taboo by going into the town in the way that I did, but that didn't really seem to matter anymore.

We continued on an uneventful patrol and I returned to the settlement with a story for everyone. Some of the guys stood there in disbelief as I recounted what had happened in the village and some just shrugged their shoulders as if to say "so what". I wanted my friends to try going into the village the same way and to see for themselves what would happen. It wasn't to be though. The next day I was in Migdalim on guard when I heard shots fired from Kutsra.

When the patrol returned I asked one if them what happened. It turned out that they had stopped outside the school and the usual ruckus had begun. One of the newer guys had urged his commander to allow him to fire into the air arguing that it would surely clear the crowd. He was eventually granted permission to do so. All the kids bolted and the disturbance dissipated. What really got to me was how flushed with happiness he was at being able to open fire. For 24 hours I had been living in a more hopeful place, naively believing that it was possible for us to get on with one another, only to have the myth shattered for me by one of my own.

38

FOX HUNTING

Mercifully, the jeep patrols were just one facet of our work while we were on line duty. Intelligence-led operations continued as before. One of the big men of Nablus during my time there was called Muhammad Nidal. We called him the Fox, because every time we'd tried to pick him up he had managed to escape. He had already spent 19 years in Israeli jails and was supposedly insistent that one way or another he would never go back. Upon his release he had gone straight back to Nablus – his familiar territory. He was involved in organising operations against settlements, against civilians and against his own people. One of his more infamous actions had been to try to assassinate the Mayor of Nablus only to miss and kill his son.

When we were first briefed for the mission I was still new to the unit. I remember feeling a flush of excitement at the thought of picking up a genuine bad guy. My enthusiasm increased after we performed a dress rehearsal on the base. We never left the base, though, as the mission was cancelled at the last minute. This was the first of many times we'd prepare to go out and get the Fox only to be stood down. It happened so often I stopped believing we'd ever actually be sent after him. Eventually, even the briefings stopped. It wasn't until we were at Migdalim that I heard the name of the Fox again.

I was doing the dishes at the time with Liran and Forrest. I was knee-deep in leftover hard-boiled eggs, cream cheese and that nasty, dry rice that only the army seems able to conjure up when the deputy head of the unit poked his head around the door. "Forget that shit, get your kit together, move to the vehicles now! We've got the Fox!" I didn't believe him and said as much. He looked at me and said, "This time it's really happening – get your stuff quickly!"

The only reason that our unit was carrying out this mission was because the IDF's equivalent of the US Navy SEALs was unable to get into the area in time. It was supposed to be their mission. I had heard that they had been preparing for it intensively. This level of terrorist was usually only apprehended by the SEALs, as the chances of running into trouble were high and they were above us in the hierarchy of elite units in the IDF. I smiled as I pictured the faces of the soldiers in the Sayeret who would be pissed that such a high-profile mission was given to us rather than them.

We came to a halt outside the building and flew out of the vehicles to our assigned positions. We knew the value of arriving at those positions quickly. The Fox was legendary for being able to smell the presence of Israelis and his network of informers had no doubt already called him. The difference between his successful apprehension and another wasted mission depended on all of us being able to take up our positions in time to stop him from making a run for it. For this reason we didn't bother forming up into one big group and making our way together. Instead every squad leader grabbed his guys and we all sprinted to our assigned positions.

I was directly behind Uzi who was serving as our squad leader and Liran was behind me. On the run I realised that something was going wrong. Uzi was making a wrong turn. "Uzi no!" In the silence of the night my whisper sounded to me like a roar. He turned and looked at me as I pointed to the left and continued in the correct direction without changing pace. It was ironic that I, officially the worst navigator in the unit, could correlate everything that I saw before me with the map I had studied at the base. We found our position and I trained my night scope on the building frantically searching the windows for the sight of a man running out the back. I saw no one. We prepared to fire at the building in a coordinated barrage by all the squads surrounding the apartment block: our wake-up call to the Fox.

The shots of the unit opening up echoed all around the street and back into us – a violent explosion of noise in the early hours of the morning. It had no apparent affect on the residents inside. They must have been woken by the shooting; they must have been scared. I saw no lights go on, nor any movement. I heard an Arabic speaker on a megaphone calling on everyone to get out of the building and present themselves and their identification to the troops waiting outside.

The seconds ticked by, they became minutes and soon I felt that I had been watching the building for a year and there was still no movement from inside. We were ordered to fire another barrage at the walls. I took the opportunity to loose off another five rounds and immediately changed magazines. I ran my scope over the building and was pleased to see that the lights inside were finally being turned on. I could hear the megaphone whine once again and the muted sounds of orders being given in a clipped Arabic could be heard coming from the other side of the building. They were beyond my sight and my responsibility; I had only one job, one very simple task. I was to look at the back of the building and shoot anyone that tried to escape. The easiest jobs somehow have a way of becoming the most difficult.

Had I been at the front of the building I would have had people with me, it would have been a position with things to do. I could have been checking IDs, searching people as they came out, and maybe finding someone who knew where the Fox was and could give us some decent intelligence. Instead, I was stuck with only two others in a semi-concealed position far removed from any of those activities. All I could do was keep my weapon trained on the building and look at it. I traced the course of the moon across the clear night sky. I looked for the North Star a dozen times and asked myself again how it was possible for it to move and yet still show me where north was. I drank water from my drinking sack, shared a nod or two with Uzi and checked behind me to make sure Liran hadn't fallen asleep. Other than that there was nothing to break the monotony of the most important mission I'd ever participated in.

I realised within the first ten minutes that the Fox wasn't in the building. No one had opened fire on us, no one had attempted to escape and all the residents had left without any trouble at all. He wasn't there. I watched the moon sink lower and lower in the sky, looked to the east and heard the call to prayer reverberate on the loudspeakers around the city at about 5 a.m. I usually measured how close we were to packing up by this mournful melody. Hanging around Nablus in the daytime was like sending out invitations to riot. I was surprised when the sun finally reared its head and we had still hadn't been given the order to leave.

Eventually the sweep of the building began. The guys hadn't moved in until a complete check had been done on all the people who had left the building to make sure we didn't have him already. Levine, Tom and Forrest moved inside with Amit and his squad backing them up. I wished I were with them; building clearance was the coolest part of a soldier's job as well as being the most dangerous. I was always the anonymous guy covering the side of the house. Occasionally we'd shoot at the house before making any moves towards it. This was when there was someone dangerous inside so they'd know not to fuck around with us. But that paled in comparison to being the one trusted to go inside and hunt the terrorist.

The sweep was being conducted slowly and I had stopped listening to the progress over the radio. I gazed upon the building before me, the crumbling structure with the dirty windows sitting in their rusting frames. There was the occasional balcony with some pot plants growing haphazardly and the odd swathe of plaster that seemed to be holding the whole thing together.

Someone reached out and closed one of the windows in its rusty frame. They closed it slowly, deliberately, carefully, on a second floor flat. I didn't say anything. I just continued to watch the window being closed through my scope. Firing on the building was a no-no owing to the presence of our own guys inside.

To my left I heard, "Was that what I thought it was?"

"Damn right" I said.

Uzi transmitted to Levine inside the building that there was someone in the second-floor apartment. It had to be him. The civilians outside had sworn there was no one left in the building even after being told that if anyone were found inside they would be treated as a threat and dealt with accordingly.

Once they had figured out exactly which apartment we were talking about they went in hard, clearing the rooms by shooting into them. No chances were taken and a grenade was tossed in for good measure. The guys moved into the apartment. They found nothing except considerable mess that had been caused by the grenade and their bullets. No body and no sign of life. They proceeded forward, towards the kitchen. Levine took out a grenade, but Forrest stopped him, pointing out that they probably used gas canisters for cooking; they compromised, entering the room guns blazing. They found nothing to suggest the Fox was or had ever been in there.

Before they could get depressed about it they heard muffled voices coming from the room that had already been cleared. They seemed to be coming from the wall itself. As they moved in to investigate they realised that the shouts were in fact coming from behind a cupboard. What confused the guys was that they could hear shouts, plural. Tom kicked the cupboard over and they pulled the guys out of a little hole behind the cupboard to be cuffed and searched. We had the Fox!

When we heard that he had been caught with someone else we congratulated each other and waited for the order to pack up. It turned out that the man he was caught with was Saloman

Tishtush. He was also on our hit list of most wanted terrorists. He was later released in the trade-off for the captured Israeli soldier Gilad Shalit who had been kidnapped from his tank and held in Gaza for several years.

The chances of a riot developing over their capture were high so we had to get to the cars quick. I watched various squads move from their covering positions to our transport. Then it was our turn. When we reached the vehicles I saw the Palestinian civilians sitting on the ground. I noticed one woman whose son was talking to her but she just stared straight ahead.

When we were in the vehicle Liran leaned over and told me the Fox was to be travelling with us in the car.

"He's coming with us?" I repeated back to him.

"Yeah, and Amit is travelling with us too."

Wow, I thought, so I was actually going to meet this guy who had orchestrated so many attacks; the one who was responsible for so many dead. The thought intimidated me. Suicide bombers were one thing but they were easy. When you turned up on their doorstep, they gave up without any problems. The Fox was something different; I was surprised we'd even managed to get him alive. Alongside my fear there was also curiosity. What did this boss of the terrorism industry look like? How would he behave around us? Mainly, I guess I just wanted to see the guy who had managed to evade us for so long.

When Motti brought him out he was shaking and crying. He was babbling non-stop in Hebrew and in Arabic. He was blindfolded, so Motti had to help him get into the car and sat him on the floor. Then he started crying again, shouting one minute that he wanted see an officer and the next begging for someone to shoot him. He went on alternatively crying and begging for death the whole time I was with him. He didn't really mean what he said about begging for death. When Forrest had pulled him and Tishtush from their hiding place they'd found a gun and plenty of ammunition with them. He had ample time to kill himself. He also had ample opportunity to start a firefight when our guys were sweeping the lower floors. He could have gone out in a blaze of glory. He chose to cry and humiliate himself instead.

Seeing him destroyed any romantic notions of the conflict I still had. I had travelled all the way from London to pick up a rifle and defend Israel because I was a Jew. I had assumed that had I been born a Palestinian I would have quickly made the decision to pick up a rifle and defend my people from the IDF. That instinct didn't explain suicide bombing but suicide bombers seemed so shell-shocked when we picked them up that I dismissed them as having been indoctrinated. I only came face to face with the difference between reality and my fairy tale notions when I met the Fox. Watching him cry in front of us while knowing that he had killed and planned on killing many more and even sending Palestinians to blow themselves up in Israel broke me. This was no contest of people in a desperate situation trying to do what they think is right. It was about a psycho who didn't believe in his cause enough to go down fighting for it.

It followed all the way down the chain. The stone throwers we took on were scummy kids taking over people's homes and throwing the contents of their own people's lives at us. Here I was meeting one of the big bosses and he hadn't fired a shot. He begged us to shoot him instead while crying his heart out.

I finally understood that Palestinian stare they always seemed to give us. It was the stare of a people who knew they were beaten. A people represented least by those who claimed to be fighting hardest for them. What would the Fox have been if he hadn't been the Fox? A grocer? A butcher? The fact that we were after him had made him into a hero in his clan, a man of power, someone whose life was filled with mystery. He preached hate and destruction but when it came time for him to pull the trigger himself, he chose a lifetime in an Israeli jail over certain death.

39

LAST TIME OUT

It was given the grand title of "Course Preparation for Civilian Life". To me it seemed like a waste of time. I had been a civilian for 22 years before joining the army so why was I now to be subjected to classroom learning on how to be one again? So I didn't go. That was what led to me receiving a phone call from my officer, waking me up, telling me that I had to go see the battalion commander at once. This was a little confusing as I was practically out of the army by now. In the eyes of the army they were doing me a favour by sending me on that course and letting me sleep in my own bed every night. Once the programme finished I was due to finish my service anyway so I hadn't thought that going AWOL would even be noticed by anyone. When I made it to the base I bumped into some guys I knew from the Sayeret who told me that a register of attendees had been taken daily on the course and that my name had been missing.

And so the bullshit began. I was shown into the big man's office, where, for the first time since boot camp, I saluted someone and began to give him my spiel. "Well sir, I didn't realise that the course was compulsory. I didn't know sir and did I mention that I am here without any family, that I don't speak Hebrew so well and and and …"

He sent me to Amit for a less formal punishment. This was both better and worse. On the one hand, the punishment was going to be less severe. On the other, there was less room to get out of it. He would see through this one with his eyes closed. So

I went back and he simply said, "You owe the army five days, and you'll do them before being released." Not unhappy with this arrangement I said, "Yes Sir, but I didn't bring clothes with me for five days so can I go back and get them?" To which he agreed. Five days became four.

The following day I arrived back at the settlement with clothing for another few days knowing that no one was going to give me any work to do and that all I had to do was sit and watch DVDs. Scratch days two and three. On day four the boys were all called together as there was an operation happening that night. I asked Levine if I could come too. I figured a nice little raid would let me finish off my time in style. The briefing was standard and I wasn't really listening. There was a bad guy on the loose and he had to be arrested, blah blah. Stuff together, final speech, in the cars, in the kasbah.

We moved toward our target. I didn't dwell on the fact that I would never be there again. I didn't know then the extent to which the place would haunt me long after I'd left. We formed up and moved out and surrounded the house. The guy wasn't home. This was also normal and I prepared to receive the order to move back to base where we would have our customary hot coffee, cigarette and get into the sleeping bag. It wasn't to be.

The operation changed from a one-off arrest. Not sure what was happening, I was informed that there wasn't going to be a chance for us to get out of there that night. We were instructed to find a safe place and wait till morning. My decision to go on one last mission was turning into a mistake. We found a beautiful house in the middle of the kasbah that was empty and took it over to wait out the situation. We sat there for about ten hours and then it was over. Just like that. The call came through on the radio that we were being extracted. We returned to base and I was out of the army.

That's how fast it happened, that's the amount of time I had to get used to the fact that my fate was once again my own. I returned the equipment I had signed for, paid the money I was fined for the equipment I had lost and I was done.

The burning question "now what?" circled its way around my head. The routine for Israelis finishing the army was to get a job for a year or so, save money and then take a trip to a distant place, usually south-east Asia or South America. There they'd go with a bunch of friends who had also just finished the army, they'd take loads of drugs and get fucked up together far away from everyone they knew and then, maybe, they'd come home again and sort out a new life as a civilian. But I wasn't Israeli, not really, and I didn't have the first idea what to do with myself now that I was done. I wondered what became of my dreams of becoming a General. Why I didn't go the route of commanders' course and officer school. At the time I had told myself that it was because I didn't want to miss any action. There was another reason. I hadn't wanted to take on the responsibility of command. I didn't have the confidence in myself that if things had gone wrong I would have known what to do. Once I was out I regretted not becoming an officer but it was too late.

There were other things too. Things that I didn't want to admit. The army had given me so much. It had instilled in me a sense of pride in myself, a feeling of achievement, and most importantly the feeling of belonging, of being a part of the country. I had learnt Hebrew in the army and I had formed bonds that neither time nor distance could break. But the army had also taken from me. My utopian vision of Israel was destroyed by the knowledge that, in fact, Israel is a real country with real people. The Israel I had landed in was a paradise under siege from all sides, defended by heroes, the bravest of the brave. Now I had seen the truth, Israel was just as beset with problems as anywhere else and the people who lived there were exactly the same as everyone else. The best were wonderful, the worst were awful, and the majority somewhere in between.

40

THE DESCENT

I was alone, sitting in my shorts and T-shirt, looking down the hill at nothing in particular. No rifle, no green uniform, no purpose. Thoughts buzzed through my head, around and around without forming into anything substantial. I had to figure out what my next move was going to be. I had the whole world lying at the foot of the hill waiting for me. I didn't want to go down. I had a feeling in the pit of my stomach; a nervous feeling of adrenaline. It sat inside my gut like a ball and it wouldn't go away. I was 25 years old and my life had already peaked. I had been engaged in counter-terrorism operations a mere month ago and now I was engaged in … nothing. There was no choice. I was out of the army and that other dimension beckoned. London.

My plane landed in the rain. It was grey and murky and I was in England again. I'd been saddened to leave Israel but I hadn't wanted to stay. So I was back to being with the family and the friends I had left behind. I had attempted to leave the kibbutz as quietly as possible. Not even saying goodbye to my adoptive family. I felt I had let them down by being such a recluse. I was disappointed in myself and unable to deal with my shattered vision of the country I had loved so much from afar. I said goodbye to a few people, unable to vocalise the words that I was so sure I would never have to utter: "I'm going home." Israel was my home, but I couldn't stay there. The land of my birth beckoned.

My brother picked me up from the airport, he drove me home to my British middle-class existence and a new struggle to fit back into the life I so happily turned my back on three years before. He handed me a joint in the car and I stayed stoned for the next few years. It took about two weeks of lying on their couch before my parents started nagging me to get a job.

The year after I set foot in England a bunch of Muslim guys born and bred in the UK blew themselves up in what has come to be known as the 7/7 terror atrocities. It made me think back to Mike's Place; the boys from Britain didn't need to head out to Israel any more, they were perfectly content blowing themselves up in the UK. I felt betrayed when shortly after the attacks that killed 52 civilians the Mayor of London Ken Livingstone equated me, and other young Jews like me, to a suicide bomber, saying:

> If a young Jewish boy in this country goes and joins the Israeli army, and ends up killing many Palestinians in operations and can come back, that is wholly legitimate. But for a young Muslim boy in this country, who might think: I want to defend my Palestinian brothers and sisters and gets involved, he is branded as a terrorist. And I think it is this that has infected the attitude about how we deal with these problems.

I had been more than willing to risk my life to stop a suicide bomber. I thought of the lives I had saved by arresting suicide bombers. The only English Muslim boys I could think of who had gone to "defend Palestine" were the ones who had strapped explosives to their bodies. They protected no one and weren't trying to, they were trying to kill civilians. In London that message was always lost in translation. The Mayor had made it clear that London wasn't home.

On the weekends I went out to various bars and clubs with the friends I had left behind years earlier. While I had been away they had all grown up and qualified as doctors, lawyers and accountants. I had little in common with them anymore and attempted to compensate by telling stories of derring-do on the streets of Nablus. But, no one had ever heard of Nablus, and once I had told them that I hadn't killed anyone, they all lost interest.

Every week we would go out, I would walk into the bar and regret the decision to leave the house. I listened to these people with their stories of tough days at the office and annoying bosses and tried to empathise, but it was hard, and I would swiftly move to the bar and drink myself stupid. Once I had run out of money for drink I would stumble around the bar, trying to look like I was having a good time until someone found me and took me home.

I worked a few temp jobs for a couple of months at a time. One was as a security guard for the same school I went to for my A levels. Everyday I'd watch the kids come in and think, "Hey, you'd better study or else you'll end up like me." I got a job with Siemens for a couple of weeks as a meter reader, which was probably my lowest point. I did a pretty good job of not letting my discomfort or misery show in the interview. At the end of our ten-minute chat we shook hands and I left the back room of the Adecco recruitment consultants and stepped onto their shop floor.

Upon stepping out of the shop into the fresh air my grin faded. I walked to my car head down focusing on the pavement before me and with my mind solely on the dreams I dared to dream when I was a child and questioning how I had failed so spectacularly to achieve any of them.

The steering wheel was hot from the sun and I couldn't quite grip it, so I just sat there for a moment or two waiting for the air conditioning to kick in. And all at once I was bathed in white light. Shaking my head I attempted to push it away, but the light was all around me. I couldn't see due to the dust that filled the air. I shook my head harder but to no avail. I looked to my right to find Forrest, but the dust was too thick. I patted my own body down but there was no blood.

The engine came to life with as much roar as a Ford Fiesta can muster and I drove away. Putting the radio on loud, I refused to check for blood on my sweaty body and drove for home and the refuge offered by my bed. The high-pitched whine remained and I could smell the dust and hear the sound of all of our boots as we raced up the steps. The four-man observation team were already there and were relieved to see us alive and well. Their commander grinned at me and whispered, "You think you had it bad?"

But I wasn't there any more. I was in London, in my car, driving home from an interview for a job to read electricity meters. We all opened fire but I couldn't see the target, I couldn't see who I was shooting at. I fired at the rooftop nonetheless. The car behind me beeped. There was no one left on the zebra crossing and several cars were waiting patiently behind me. I put the car into gear and drove on. I moved and turned into my parents' drive, ran into the house and took myself to bed looking for the release of sleep.

I got the meter-reading job and did the two-week-long course and passed the test at the end. I was given a car, a little computer gizmo, a high visibility jacket and an ID card asserting that I was an authorised meter reader for Siemens. I lost the ID card on my first day and the charger they gave me for the computer didn't work. I was left an answerphone message telling me to drive to a certain place to pick up a new one. Instead I found myself screaming down the phone to my new boss. I screamed and I shouted about the cable and I went back to my bed and the escape from life provided by sleep.

The next day I was forced to drive outside London and apologise to the man who had hired me. I was given the new cable and sent on my way. I found myself roaming various streets of London, entering into people's homes and pretending to read their meters. I had to pretend – I didn't know how to do it having been too engaged in flashbacks during the course to pay any attention in class. I arrived at one house and rang the bell. The lady of the house answered and in I went to find that her meter sat high up on a wall. She handed me a chair and I climbed up. I heard the cracking in my ears but I ignored it. The deep pops of a heavy machine gun and the higher-pitched snaps of Kalashnikovs. The woman started speaking to me. "Last month we were overcharged on our electricity."

I ignored her but she persisted. "I called them, I was standing here and I called them with my husband. You know, they said they were going to refund us our money but we haven't heard anything from them."

The gunshots were getting louder and M16s were kicking in too with their more measured single shots. The sounds melded together into an impenetrable white noise. I couldn't quite see the numbers properly and was straining to on my tiptoes. "Did they send you to give me my money back?" she asked. I didn't reply until I heard "Excuse me!" to which I looked down at this middle-aged blonde lady who had her hands on her overstuffed hips looking up at me as if I was a naughty child.

"Er, no," I responded and returned to the meter, but the computer wasn't letting me input the numbers. An error message kept coming up on the screen telling me I was doing it wrong. It was so hot. I wanted to throw the thing on the floor and jump on top of it. Instead I just looked back and started all over again. The woman kept on complaining about her electricity bills. I was struck by a deafening roar and a blinding white light. I looked to see if Forrest was ok. All I saw was this woman looking up at me.

I assured her I would pass her complaint on to the electric company. Outside the sun was still shining. I had only been in there for a couple of minutes. I was shaking and sat down on the side of the road looking at the ground. The guns had stopped and the white light was gone. I rubbed my eyes to clear away my tears of frustration. I couldn't understand how it was that I had found myself back in London listening to old women talk about electricity bills. It wasn't supposed to be this way. I was supposed to be a hero. I was supposed to have become a General.

I spent a lot of time sleeping during those months. Life just didn't seem worth living any more. For as long as I could remember I had wanted to be a Paratrooper. Now I had done it I had no other ambition. My former passion for Israel had been, if not extinguished, at least weakened by all I had seen over the past two years. Yet contradictorily my service remained something I was more proud of than anything else I'd ever done. So much so, that I yearned to go back. I missed my friends. I missed carrying a rifle and going out into the Nablus night. I missed doing something I felt was important, something that affected people's lives. I had gone from being trusted to operate equipment worth millions of dollars to failing to read people's electricity meters because I didn't know how to use the equipment.

I kept thinking about Liran and Uzi and the others. I kept wishing I was back with them. I dreamt of being able to put the uniform back on and go out into the night with them. I remembered a comic I had read years before about a Vietnam war veteran who died and in death was reunited with his squad from Vietnam. They fought a permanent war together. It was something I wished for from my bedroom in London.

I was drunk as often as possible. One night I came home and threw up in my room on the floor. I screamed and shouted at my parents until they locked themselves in their room. I would go out and drink myself into a stupor and then run through the contacts in my phone and shout at them about nothing. I was in pain and I couldn't understand why. I felt guilty about that pain; I hadn't been in a 'real' war, no one I knew had been killed, so how could I justify the flashbacks and the discomfort? There was no point to anything. There was no reason to go out and earn money. There was nothing I wanted. Except to go back and I didn't understand why I wanted that either – everyone I had served with had desperately wanted to get out.

I couldn't help but lament against the fact that one minute

I was trusted with the lives of my entire unit each night as I walked behind them covering them. I was respected, admired, even loved by those around me and everyone who saw me wearing my red beret. I was defending a grateful nation. The next day I was in another country armed with a BA in History that no one cared about and a few stories no one wanted to hear. And it was my choice. It was my choice to go in the first place and it was my choice to return to London. So how was it that everything felt so wrong?

They say that a hugely disproportionate number of London's homeless people are ex-servicemen. It's easy to understand why. After the army nothing had any zest to it. There was no challenge. Instead of acting in the name of great ideals like freedom and the protection of a nation you're doing nothing other than looking after yourself. I had earned jump wings and a red beret. I knew how to fire an antitank missile, I could field strip an M4 rifle and I could pick up and fire a whole bunch of machine guns. But because I couldn't use Microsoft Excel or lacked a couple of years experience making people coffee in an office I was useless.

I was so angry and so unsure how to deal with any of it. I yearned, begged and prayed to go back to Nablus. To spend every night on ops with my friends, to never stop, to never leave, never move on. Years later I told this to Uzi and he cut me off: "You wished you'd died there a hero so you could live forever." He knew to say that because he felt it too.

One night I found myself kneeling on the ground outside my parent's house. I was with a friend and had been talking about moving through Nablus. I knelt down on one knee, invisible rifle in my hands. I was explaining how you use the walls and have to make sure to keep as much of your body hidden as possible. I looked up at him. He was looking up the other side of the street and back towards the house as if worried someone would see us. He wasn't listening. I looked back down the street while kneeling there, looked down at my empty hands. Hands with no rifle in them. I saw the nice houses, with trees planted every so often, and lamp posts with their orange light. I stood up. "C'mon let's go back inside," I said. He flicked his cigarette away and we went back towards the house. "Did you ever watch The Office?" he asked. "No," I said. "I haven't seen it, mate."

One day I woke up and saw death sitting on the windowsill. Only he didn't look like the grim reaper; he looked like a court jester with a white face and that hat with a bell on each droopy tip. He told me to open the window and just jump out. It wasn't that high but if I went out headfirst I could probably make sure it was all over. I saw him sitting there. I heard his voice in my head. His offer was tempting. It could all be over. I could end the misery; spare my parents my drunken rants. Israel was a dimension away. The army was gone and even if I went back in it wouldn't be the same. Those of my friends who hadn't got out were on their way out. Sometimes I wondered if I had ever been there at all.

Within all of this I looked at death sitting there on my window. He hadn't come to me as an enemy but as a friend. He wasn't to be feared but to be greeted warmly. It was strange for him to just be sitting there offering me a way out. I didn't take it. I rose from the bed and walked to the window. He wasn't there anymore. I opened it and looked down at the ground. If I wanted to go I really would have to go head first, I doubted it would be enough of a drop to kill me. I didn't take the easy way out. I guess that was what people call rock bottom. But there was light at the end of the tunnel. I decided I didn't want to die.

41

THE ROAD BACK

I went to therapy. It helped. A very little bit. Once I had decided I didn't want to die decisions to improve things seemed to come along quite quickly. I quit smoking skunk. Then I quit smoking weed altogether. I never quit drinking. I never quit going crazy when I drank. But then some vices you hold onto more tightly than others. I did a diploma in journalism. I took a Masters in War Studies. I got a job. I got my shit together. Slowly. Over a period of three years I went down to rock bottom and brought myself back up again.

While studying for my Masters war broke out between Israel and Lebanon. My team, recently released from the regular army into the reserves were all called up. Some were out of the country but those who weren't were thrust once again into the breech. The guilt clawed at me again. They were there while I was in London studying. I called them as much as I could before they slogged their way over the border and into some Lebanese village. There they sat, until they left. Liran told me there was nothing for them to do there. They sat. Mortars were fired at them. They withdrew. He said, "You put your helmet on tight, lie down and hope nothing hits you." I felt like a fraud. A real war comes along and I sit well out of it in London. Their stories of tramping over the border, getting mortared and then tramping back again after achieving nothing brought the army back into focus. There's no such thing as a "real" war.

I never stopped worrying and I never stopped wishing I was back in Nablus with my brothers, repeating the same mission. It didn't matter which one, so long as we were all together moving through the night.

I never regretted joining the army. People said sometimes that it must have changed me – a cliché that did nothing but annoy me. Sure it changed me, but only in ways I didn't understand and educated me in skills that weren't useful. Being able to take apart an M16 and put it back together again didn't mean much in job interviews. Saying I had been in the Israeli army didn't mean anything save for the fact that I had no experience of whatever job it was I was applying for. The security job, the meter reading and all the other jobs were just things I did while trying to figure out what on earth was going on. As if gravity no longer functioned in the same way and I needed to get used to moving around walking upside down. But I got used to it.

In 2010 I moved back to Israel but this time I just moved to a country called Israel. I didn't move to a paradise, a place of milk and honey or some kind of holy place the Messiah was imminently arriving to. I was going back to the land and country of my people. Dirty, dusty, imperfect but ours.

I never found my battlefield of glory. My redemption in fields of fire never came. In 2012 I was on standby to be thrown into Gaza and in 2014 I watched the fighting in Gaza unfold on television and ran to cower in bomb shelters when the sirens wailed. My wife ran from buses that stopped in the middle of the road and lay flat on the ground, hoping not to get hit. I first met Uzi's little brother when he was a 7-year-old kid. In 2014 I watched him go to fight in Gaza.

People often say about Israel 'so what's the answer?' as if Israel is a question or a riddle in need of a solution. Israel is a country. A country at war. Maybe, hopefully, one day her wars will end. Until they do we'll keep fighting them. The time I was there, the time I served, this is what the fighting looked like. When it was Uzi's brother's turn it looked different and today it has probably changed yet again. But the country is still there and for some strange reason people think that that isn't an answer in and of itself.

If you ask me whether it was worth it my answer is yes.

CPSIA information can be obtained
at www.ICGtesting.com
Printed in the USA
LVHW082211061019
633367LV00015B/871/P